THE GREAT GOD OF MEN

REFLECTIONS ON THE PATH TO SPIRITUAL MATURITY

.

JEFF BIANCHI

DEDICATION

To my lovely wife Sarah - You are my greatest gift on earth. Thank you for being my heart companion for the rest of life. I love you "whole, city, world!"

TABLE OF CONTENTS

ACKNOWLEDGEMENTS

To Jude Knight – I love you, my son. May you grow up to love Jesus with all of your heart; and may you be the worshipper of God and the deliverer of men that He has called you to be.

To Jake Saint – I love you, my son. May you carry the Father's heart and extend it to the needy world around you.

To Mike O'quin – You are a true example of a man. The challenge to write a book was just the encouragement I needed.

To John Clark – You have been an incredible support in life and in this entire project. You are a faithful servant and a dear friend.

To Kurt Mahler – I am so grateful for all the time you put into this project. You are a master wordsmith and this book is far better because of your input.

To Jenna Tourje – Thanks for looking over this manuscript and polishing it up. You were a true gift and an answer to prayer for me in this book writing process.

To Adam Reed – Thank you for your design work on the cover. You are a true son in the faith. I am proud of you.

To Jiness Skeete – Jesus is truly the Resurrection and the Life. I can't wait to join you as we dance on the streets of gold someday!

To my parents – Thank you so much for praying for me and providing for me throughout my life and for always believing in me. I love you.

To Lisa – Thank you for praying for and believing for me through the rough times and for your consistency in your relationship with God. I am glad to be your brother.

To Jimmy, Mark and Joe – Thank you for being friends and mentors who believed in me at all times and taught me what it means to be a leader. I love you men a ton.

To Sean and Laura – Thank you so much for loving well and helping to restore my confidence in God and His goodness. I look forward to the day we rock in our chairs together saying, "We completed what He gave us to do!"

To my CFCF family – It is a great honor to be your leader. You are the best community in the world! I'm looking forward to the years to come.

To my CFI family – It is such a joy to be a part of this lean, mean, loving machine of a movement of churches. Thanks for all the risks that you have made to make Jesus known!

To my AMI family – I am so glad to know what my tribe is! I'm committed for life to proclaim Jesus with my band of brothers and sisters.

To the Lord Jesus Christ – Thank you for being the great God of men and never giving up on me! I love You forever because You first loved me.

PREFACE

Three years ago, on a spring day in Boston, a friend of mine, Mike, looked straight at me and said, "You should write a book. I think you have it in you." At first I was taken aback by this statement and did not have a strong vision for writing. However, as I began to consider this, a latent desire was awakened in me.

As I began to think through what I would want to write about, I reflected on the experience of God's faithfulness in my life. A theme emerged that put words to the experience of my family and friends in ministry over the past two decades. It was this: When all is said and done, it is not about the great men of God, but the great God of those men. It is not primarily our faithfulness to Him, but His incredible faithfulness to us. My mind turned to the ways God had interacted with His people throughout the biblical narrative, and as a result, I began to write this book.

Another desire that developed within me as I was writing this book was to preserve a piece of the history of our larger family of churches at Antioch Ministries International based in Waco, Texas, and Community of Faith International in Boston, Massachusetts. It was also an opportunity to honor some of the people who have played a part in seeing us become who we are today. Each person has a unique perspective and a story to tell and I wanted to reflect on God's faithfulness by looking at the lives that I have come in contact with along the way.

An issue that I would like to address at this point is the usage of the word *men* in the book title, as well as the fact that no women are mentioned in the section titles. While the term *men* seems to be dismissive of women, don't let this confuse you. The term *men* refers to God's relationship to mankind as a whole, men as well as women. This book tells the stories of numerous women, and without recounting their contribution to the history of the church and our movement, this book would be woefully incomplete.

The overall purpose in writing this book is to observe the lives of these biblical figures and stories from the history of our movement, and to reflect upon the lessons that can be learned from them. God is faithful, and His desire is for us to grow to full maturity in our faith in Him. However, many obstacles present themselves along the path of righteousness and an understanding of God's ways in maturing us is essential in order not to become disheartened by difficulty, embittered by disappointment, or entangled by worldliness. By reflecting on these lessons, I desire to help those who read this book to finish the race well and to grow to full maturity in their faith.

This book is divided into thirty-one chapters. Feel free to read it straight through or to use it devotionally. Whether this is my first and only offering remains to be seen. However, I pray that this book will be used by God to increase our desire to know Him and expand His kingdom for the rest of our lives.

Jeff Bianchi – June 2012

INTRODUCTION
THE PATH TO MATURITY

God has been a million times
better to me than I have been to him.
- D.L Moody, 19th century evangelist

This book is written with the hope of increasing our desire to respond to God's divine initiations with us, and to help us avoid the pitfalls that sabotage our ability to mature in Him. Modern-day Christianity has often been self-absorbed, prioritizing our comforts, rights, and blessings. The path to spiritual maturity, however, leads to a decreased self-obsession and an increased devotion to God. As we grow in faith, we increasingly understand the truth that *"He is the one and his name will be the only one"* (Zechariah 14:9). This book is not written primarily about the great men of God in the Bible, but about the greatness of the God who called those men. I am awed by the limitless patience of God in my own life in light of the countless self-centered decisions I have made. He has not allowed me to be destroyed by my willful and stubborn ways, nor has He given me up to the sin that I have so foolishly embraced. His mercy has triumphed over judgment countless times in my life and His incredible faithfulness has begun to build in me a life of consistency in Him. My testimony is the same as a myriad of unknown believers throughout history, and it is my desire to write on their behalf.

During a prayer meeting I attended a number of years ago, a young lady described a divine picture of a beautiful marriage ceremony. The bride stood behind the closed doors of the sanctuary in a stunning wedding dress and was preoccupied with the details and beauty of her garments. While looking at the pearls and elaborate embroidery of her sleeve, she touched one of them in wonderment. The doors suddenly swung open and she went down the aisle obsessed with her appearance.

About halfway down the aisle, however, she looked up and her eyes caught sight of the groom. The moment she saw his handsome face and loving gaze, she was overwhelmed. All of her self-preoccupation melted away and she walked the rest of the way up the aisle confident, because her eyes were on him. He was all that mattered, for she knew he had completely accepted her. This is a wonderful picture of the process of maturing in our relationship with God. In the initial stages of discipleship, we are not lovers of God, but lovers of ourselves. As we pursue Him, though, in the course of time it ceases to be all about us. What we desire most is to be with Him, to see Him, and to bring Him glory through our lives.

In the Book of Jeremiah we read:

> *This is what the Lord says: "Let not the wise man boast of his wisdom, or the strong man boast of his strength, or the rich man boast of his riches, but let him who boasts boast about this:* that he understands and knows me, *that I am the Lord, who exercises kindness, justice and righteousness on earth, for in these I delight."* (Jeremiah 9:23-24, emphasis added)

In our contemporary culture, we are enamored with celebrities and personalities. Even in the Christian world, we tend toward exalting men and worshipping them as "heroes." The one whom we should desire to have among us, more than any famous athlete or influential person, however, is Jesus. He is the only one we absolutely cannot do without. My hope for this book is to enlarge our capacity to love God and to empower us to revel in His amazing grace. On the appointed day, when the clouds are finally parted, we will be overwhelmed that we knew so little of the Almighty One. Let us give the rest of our lives to the pursuit of the Great God of Men!

SECTION 1

CHOSEN

*God, I pray Thee, light these idle sticks of my
life and may I burn for Thee. Consume my life,
my God, for it is Thine. I seek not a long life,
but a full one, like you, Lord Jesus.*
- Jim Elliot, Missionary and martyr in Ecuador

While He was with His disciples, Jesus declared, *"You did
not choose me, but I chose you and appointed you to go and
bear fruit-fruit that will last. Then the Father will give you
whatever you ask in my name"* (John 15:16). God is the
initiator and we are given a choice to respond to His
promptings. Maturing in our faith is the process by which we
learn to respond to God's divine initiations. We enter the
Christian life by believing in Christ alone for our salvation.
This starting point is sometimes referred to as "our first love".
But God's ultimate intention is that we finish the journey more
in love with Him than when we began. It is not His desire that
we grow tired or succumb to worldliness, bitterness or fear. He
wants us to move forward in our faith, from one degree of His
glory to the next. In the book of Exodus we read, *"Although
Moses was one-hundred and twenty years old when he died,
his eye was not dim, nor his vigor abated"* (Exodus 34:7 -
NASB). Moses was strong to the end, having learned God's
lessons and having overcome the enemy of his soul. May God
work in us what is pleasing to Him as we reflect on the lives of
those whom He chose.

5

CHAPTER 1

THE ONE WHOM GOD CHOOSES: A LOOK AT THE JUDGES OF ISRAEL

The Israelites endured an extremely dark period following the conquest of the Promised Land and they were unable to break out of a vicious cycle of sin and depravity. God, the merciful one, sought deliverance for unfaithful Israel time and again through the different men and women He chose. A thorough reading of the Book of Judges, however, presents compelling proof that God has a sense of humor. Could a less impressive group have been called upon to bring deliverance? As humans, we naturally select people who increase our odds of success. Take a pickup game of basketball, for example. Before the game begins, a pecking order is established. While each one shoots and dribbles, the other players evaluate his or her talent level. Two people eventually surface as the leaders and begin to pick the members of their teams. We less skilled ones who have experienced this ritual know the sense of trepidation as one after the other is selected to play while we are still waiting to be chosen.

But God did not look with human eyes when He chose individuals to fulfill His purpose for the nation of Israel. Even up to the present day, He is looking for weak vessels who choose to obey Him and let Him shine through their lives. He pursues the broken, the weak, and the despised, and calls them to do great exploits. Paul exhorted the believers in Corinth:

> Brothers, think of what you were when you were called: Not many of you were wise by human standards; not many were influential; not many were of noble birth. But God chose the foolish things of the world to shame the wise; God chose the weak things of the world to shame the strong. He chose the lowly things

of the world and the despised things—and the
things that are not—to nullify the things that
are, so that no one may boast before him. (1
Corinthians 1:26-29)

Our God delights to shame the wise with foolish things.
With Him, the last one chosen ends up making the game
winning shot.

Consider Ehud, a Benjamite who was God's choice to lead
Israel in Judges 3. He was a left-handed man, a seemingly
insignificant detail that revealed much about Ehud. A left-
hander in the Middle-Eastern culture of Ehud's time was a
misfit. The left hand was considered unclean and was not to be
used for eating, shaking hands, or a host of other human
interactions. A left-hander also carried the stigma that he was
likely a thief. Being a left-handed person myself, I have
experienced a few unintended persecutions even in an
accepting society. For instance, while I was learning to play
guitar, I discovered that left-handers had very few instrumental
options and I soon submitted to the right-handed world. This
may account for the inordinate amount of time it has taken me
to learn to play this instrument with any measure of grace. But
Ehud was not merely inconvenienced by being a left-handed
person. He was a man who was different - a social outcast who
endured scorn as part of his everyday life. The living God,
however, did not look down and see a potential thief, but a
potential deliverer. Ehud lived with rejection his entire life, yet
God accepted him and called him for a great mission. Ehud
would prove to be a powerful instrument of God's deliverance.

Think about Deborah, who was chosen to rule Israel
several decades later (Judges 4), and further testified to God's
amazing grace. In our Western society, it seems appalling that
women would not be treated with respect and consideration,
but in Deborah's time women were considered property. They
were often used in business transactions – fathers gave their
daughters in marriage in order to secure peace between two

groups. It was not of primary importance that a woman loved the man to whom she was given because her rights were rarely considered. But Deborah was not merely property to God; she was a person of great value. She was not unimportant to Him; she was the apple of His eye (Psalm 17:8). As such, God chose Deborah to rule with Him and rescue His people.

When God became a man in the person of Jesus, He modeled this same attitude of love and respect toward women. Jesus elevated the position of the women He encountered through His interactions with them. He treated them with respect and honor and they left His presence with a greater measure of dignity and hope. Jesus spoke to the Samaritan woman at the well, attempting to reconcile her to God (John 4). This shocked His disciples, but was consistent with God's character throughout history. After a woman who was caught in the act of adultery was brought to Him by a group of self-righteous men, He disarmed the men, forgave the woman and set her free (John 8). And in sharp contrast to the Pharisees, Jesus loved and accepted the woman with the alabaster jar who came to Him and wept at His feet (Luke 7). Those seated with Him despised her and doubted His piety, yet Jesus rebuked these men for their hardness of heart and unbelief. Jesus displayed, in human flesh, the love God has possessed for women from the beginning of creation. This extravagant love was lavished upon Deborah, and she ruled in God's name for the sake of Israel.

Imagine Gideon, hiding from Israel's Midianite oppressors (Judges 6). Gideon came from Manasseh, the smallest tribe of Israel, and considered himself to be the least important member of his tribe. Yet the angel of the Lord appeared to him as he was threshing wheat. We read, *"When the angel of the LORD appeared to Gideon, he said, 'The LORD is with you, mighty warrior'"* (Judges 6:12). This messenger defined how Gideon was known from the viewpoint of heaven. The angel saw Gideon's weakness and fear, but he also saw Who had called him mighty warrior, and God's opinion was all that mattered. It took a while for Gideon to reconcile this in his heart, but he finally surrendered to God's command to deliver Israel.

The Lord reduced Gideon's army from over thirty thousand men to a mere three hundred soldiers making it absolutely impossible for Gideon to prevail without divine intervention. During the reduction process, those soldiers who were fearful were asked to leave because they were a hindrance to God's purpose in delivering the Israelites. This proves that we should not first seek more people to do God's work, but more of God's presence because He is the only true deliverer. After this substantial weakening (to the human eye) of the Israelite army, Gideon's outnumbered troops were enabled to soundly defeat the army of the Midianites. It was not Gideon's pedigree that was important, but Who had called him. When the odds in life are insurmountable, and what God has called us to do seems far beyond our abilities, we can learn from Gideon how to approach the battle.

We should recall these biblically based truths on a regular basis:

> Great is the God who has called me.
> He calls me a mighty warrior.
> I can face the impossible in His name.
> He will deliver me,
> And many people through me.
> It is His delight to give me the kingdom.

We turn next to Jephthah, the Gileadite (Judges 11). He was a son of a prostitute, a half-breed Israelite, rejected by his own brothers and sent to a foreign country. How deep the wounds must have been that were inflicted upon his spirit at a young age. He was a man who never felt worthy, one who was relegated to the outer fringes of society and was not accepted, even by his family. With no one as an advocate, he learned to defend himself by fighting, and became an expert in combat.

But God searched throughout Israel and chose Jepththah as a man to establish peace. He experienced that blessing of which the Psalmist spoke, *"A father to the fatherless and a defender of widows is God in his holy dwelling"* (Psalm 68:5). When the time came for God to deliver Israel again from the Ammonites, his brothers pleaded with him to come back and fight for Israel's deliverance as their ruler. The chronicle of Jephthah's life demonstrates that those who are the least in man's eyes are often chosen to become the greatest in God's kingdom (Matthew 19:30).

Finally, the most famous judge of all, Samson, was born out of human weakness (Judges 13). His mother, Manoah's wife, was unable to have children. It was a physical impossibility that God made possible by His almighty power. Samson, the miracle baby, was called from birth to be a Nazirite set apart for God's holy purpose. But the gift of strength that God gave Samson in order to deliver Israel was one of the main causes of his dramatic downfall. He did not know how to properly manage this gift, and his physical prowess deceived him into thinking he was invincible. He was indeed as strong as an ox, in one battle alone killing one thousand Philistines with the jawbone of a donkey (Judges 15:15), but he was not as morally strong. Samson was eventually overcome by his unchecked predilection for women. He could conquer any foe, but he could not conquer his own passions. Samson gave in to his lust for a prostitute and later was defeated through his relationship with his wife Delilah (Judges 16), who was acting as a double agent for his Philistine enemies. Samson's experience illustrates that whatever sin pattern we are not committed to destroying will eventually destroy us.

God allowed Samson to reach the end of his own strength before the greatest victory was won. After the Philistines had captured Samson and put out his eyes, he was brought before the Philistine rulers to perform for them. Blind Samson, in a single act at his death, destroyed more Philistines than he had killed over the entire course of his life (Judges 16). Through Samson's story, God also reveals that His greatest work through us is reserved for that time when there is nothing of our own natural strength left to depend on.

We catch a glimpse of God's heart in choosing His deliverers by looking at the lives of these judges in Israel's history. Likewise, He has chosen us, not based on our strength or abilities, but simply because He loves us. With that assurance, we know that as we respond to Him, we will succeed in that which He has called us to do.

CHAPTER 2

CHOSEN TO MAKE DISCIPLES

David's First Disciples

By the time David was reigning in Jerusalem as the king of Israel, he had a powerful team surrounding him. His warriors were known as "David's mighty men" (2 Samuel 23). They were an elite group of heroes with no equal in the entire land. The star athletes of their day, they performed great exploits and each one was skilled in the art of war. One of these warriors, Josheb-Basshebeth killed eight hundred men in one encounter. A few of them had killed lions and bears, and others had killed giants. An account of three leaders of David's mighty men asserts:

> At that time David was in the stronghold, and the Philistine garrison was at Bethlehem. David longed for water and said, "Oh, that someone would get me a drink of water from the well near the gate of Bethlehem!" So the three mighty men broke through the Philistine lines, drew water from the well near the gate of Bethlehem and carried it back to David. But he refused to drink it; instead, he poured it out before the LORD. "Far be it from me, O LORD, to do this!" he said. "Is it not the blood of men who went at the risk of their lives?" And David would not drink it. Such were the exploits of the three mighty men. (2 Samuel 23:14-17)

These leaders, along with the rest of the mighty men formed a ring of fire around David to protect him day and night, and they were fully committed to his success.

Yet this is vastly different from how leadership training began for David. Long before he was king, while he was fleeing from King Saul and living in the desert, David had a different team. What a pitiful, ragtag team it was! Scripture records, *"All those who were in distress or in debt or discontented gathered around him, and he became their leader. About four hundred men were with him"* (1 Samuel 22:2). It tires me just thinking of this motley crew - people in crisis, men being pursued by creditors, and souls full of discontent. This was a difficult, painful, and yet wonderful teaching experience for the future king. The Lord established David's ability to lead by teaching him to inspire this group of misfits to become mighty men. After David was through training them, they were full of faith and ready to conquer any foe. These men found themselves in difficult situations before they were with David because they lacked discipleship. David made devoted disciples out of defeated men because he was persistent in training and modeling for them what it meant to know and live wholeheartedly for God.

Committed to Disciple-Making

Similar to how David discipled his mighty men, Jesus commanded us in the Great Commission (Matthew 28:18-20) to go and make disciples, not merely converts. Could a major reason for the lack of integrity in the contemporary Western church be due to the emphasis on numbers rather than disciples? Some leaders have not learned the accountability of taking care of a small group of people before taking charge of a large crowd. God desires for multitudes to be brought into His kingdom, and I am personally believing God for great numbers of people to be affected through my life. However, I do not want to sacrifice integrity and discipleship for the idol of numbers and bigness. In our Western context, one of the first questions asked of a pastor is, "How many people go to your church?" While this is a fair question, I suggest that a better one may be, "How many disciples of Jesus are you impacting?" I want to be sensitive to the needs of those who are coming to our church seeking God, but I do not primarily want to be "seeker-friendly." I want to be God-friendly in worship, prayer and in loving acts toward others. Through this God-friendliness we will be endued with power to seek and to save the lost. At times, gaining numbers of people without them possessing a depth of heart can be a temptation. In the long run, however, cultivating an environment of intense devotion to God is the only way that we will penetrate the darkness and spread God's kingdom to the four corners of the earth.

As a church planter, I firmly believe that Christ, through the local church is the hope of the world. Church planting is a surefire way to reveal your true motives and to put your theories of discipleship to the test. When starting from scratch, you cannot just fade into the background. The responsibility of embodying what you want to see the new church become cannot be passed off to someone else. The attributes of faith, diligence, zeal, and patience are needed in ever-increasing measures. We often remind our church planters throughout the world that if it were easy to start a movement, everyone would be doing it. Church planting requires that we continually get back to the basics and stay fresh in our relationship with Jesus. To a church that Paul himself planted, he pronounced, *"But we have this treasure in jars of clay to show that this all-surpassing power is from God and not from us"* (2 Corinthians 4:7). After more than two decades in ministry, I have a deeper understanding of this scripture because I am becoming increasingly aware of my human weakness. Yet I am not crushed, but more assured than ever of his ability to use a vessel that is completely yielded to Him.

Gladys Aylward, a British parlor maid who lived in the early 20th century, had been rejected by several Christian agencies and was not considered to be missionary material. As a result, she spent her life savings to travel from England to

China on her own. She boarded a one-way train from Europe through Siberia and finally arrived in China after a short stay in Japan. Gladys assisted an older woman named Jeannie Lawson in the town of Yuncheng in the Shaanxi Province and she eventually took over the work of the Inn of the Eight Happinesses (renamed "The Inn of the Sixth Happiness" for the movie based on her life). God later used her in a powerful way when she became a "foot inspector" who implemented the new decree against foot binding, a cruel age-old practice forced upon young women in China. She also put down a prison riot in Yuncheng after officials were unable to bring peace. Finally, during the Second World War, she led many children through a mountain range to safety in the city of Xi'an. In an interview during her later years, she had expressed her surprise at God's call to serve Him in China given her educational limitations. She confided, "I wasn't God's first choice for what I've done for China. There was somebody else...I don't know who it was — God's first choice. It must have been a man — a wonderful man. A well-educated man. I don't know what happened. Perhaps he died. Perhaps he wasn't willing...and God looked down...and saw Gladys Aylward."[1]

Let us praise God for His greatness and for calling us to join with Him to bring deliverance to many. Our hearts should be thrilled that God has chosen us to be a part of the amazing work that He is doing in the world. The victory is in realizing that the great God of men has called us to great things and He will do them as we keep our eyes on Him.

SECTION 2

ABRAHAM – MAN OF THE PROMISE

*I have held many things in my hands, and
I have lost them all; but whatever I have
placed in God's hands, that I still possess.
- Corrie Ten Boom, Author of "The Hiding Place"*

Abram, while living in the city of Haran in Ur of the Chaldeans (Babylonia), heard God speak to him one day saying *"Leave your country, your people, and your father's household and go to the place where I will show you"* (Genesis 12:1). The first missionary call in biblical history required Abram (later renamed Abraham) to walk in faith – quite literally in his non-mechanized age – to gain the promise that God had given him. God commanded him to forsake everything familiar and boldly venture into the unknown. Without taking this God-ordained risk there would have been no reward for our father in the faith. He was a righteous man because he believed the promise of God (Genesis 15:16). In our own journey with God, we rarely see the end of the path that He has marked out for us. We must follow His voice and trust that our way will become clear as we move forward in faith. The scriptures affirm, *"The path of the righteous is like the first gleam of dawn, shining ever brighter until the full light of day"* (Proverbs 4:18). God often leads one step at a time, but for those who choose to follow, He promises that He will be with them wherever the path leads. As we obey and take the next step that God is calling us to take, He will continue to reveal Himself and lead us with His presence in the most wonderful way.

CHAPTER 3

LISTENING TO HIS VOICE, SEEING WITH HIS EYES

Listening to His Voice

What must have passed through Abraham's mind as God spoke to him? Would he obey the voice telling him to leave the comforts of the familiar and risk all for the sake of his God? This would be the first in a series of tests in Abraham's life, all of which required him to do something completely against his ingrained human reasoning. In order to follow, Abraham had to forsake the idols of his father's house. The necessity of this act of radical obedience is later explained by the prophet Jonah, who wrote, *"Those who cling to worthless idols forfeit the grace that could be theirs"* (Jonah 2:8). The familiar can act as a shackle upon us that prevents forward progress in our relationship with God. We tend to gravitate toward the shallow end of the spiritual pool in an attempt to "play it safe." It is only when we get beyond what we can control and leap into the impossible that we will see the miraculous work of God. When we pass these tests of faith, as did Abraham, we will graduate to the greater things that God has in store for us. Areas such as finances, career and family require full surrender and a willingness to risk in order that the purpose of God may be fully realized in our lives.

Jackie Pullinger has called Hong Kong home since 1966 when, as a young woman, God told her to leave England and go to serve Him as a missionary. There was only one problem: no missionary organization would support her. After receiving advice from a trusted pastor, she decided to purchase a ticket on a boat going around the world, not stopping until God showed her where to disembark. Jackie, like Abraham thousands of years before, had only the promise that God would be with her. When she arrived at the port in Hong Kong, the next piece of the puzzle was revealed. God told her to go ashore, and led her to the Walled City in Hong Kong where over 30,000 people, mostly drug addicts, prostitutes, and gang members lived in an area only 31,000 yards square. It was a filthy place that even the police avoided as a result of the overwhelming corruption. There were only two toilets on ground level for all of those living in the Walled City and many people threw excrement out of their windows due to the lack of plumbing and sewage treatment. One of the names for this place in Chinese literally meant, "darkness."

As Jackie began to teach at a school in the Walled City, she was overcome with discouragement because of the hopeless plight of these people, especially the youth. Yet through trusting God and doing what she termed "unstructured youth-work", she saw hundreds of heroin addicts delivered from drugs and given new life though faith in Christ. Many also received the spiritual gift of tongues, which enabled them to painlessly withdraw from heroin, the relentless drug called "The Dragon."[2]

The Walled City was torn down in 1993 and the Hong Kong government eventually approached Jackie to ask for help because of the great success that she had experienced in seeing addicts delivered. This simple yet faith-filled woman continues to serve the poor in Hong Kong to this day. Many countless men and women whose lives have been eternally changed stand as a testimony to Jackie Pullinger's willingness to follow God's voice no matter the cost. She has a place among that great cloud of witnesses who followed in the footsteps of faith that our father Abraham walked in when he set out in obedience to God. Many voices today urge us to take the road of ease and comfort, but without a willingness to listen to divine promptings, there will be no reward. May we have the courage to take the road less travelled when our Father's voice speaks to our hearts.

Seeing With His Eyes

Abraham's nephew Lot accompanied him on the journey from Haran to Canaan along with all of their flocks and herds. When they arrived at their destination, quarrelling arose between Lot's herdsmen and the herdsman of Abraham. The account is as follows:

> *So Abram said to Lot, "Let's not have any quarreling between you and me, or between your herdsmen and mine, for we are brothers. Is not the whole land before you? Let's part company. If you go to the left, I'll go to the right; if you go to the right, I'll go to the left." Lot looked up and saw that the whole plain of the Jordan was well watered, like the garden of the LORD, like the land of Egypt, toward Zoar. (This was before the LORD destroyed Sodom and Gomorrah.) So Lot chose for himself the whole plain of the Jordan and set out toward the east. The two men parted company: Abram lived in the land of Canaan, while Lot lived among the cities of the plain and pitched his tents near Sodom. Now the men of Sodom were wicked and were sinning greatly against the LORD.* (Genesis 13:8-13)

In settling this dispute between their herdsmen, Abraham exhibited humility and godly trust. He allowed his nephew to have first choice in the division of the land. Lot looked out over the countryside and he saw that the whole plain of the Jordan was well watered. It does not say that Lot inquired of the Lord as to where he should choose to settle. Instead, he chose that which looked good to his natural eyes and was certain that he had made the right decision. Later on, however, we find out that Lot took up residence in Sodom and found himself surrounded by depravity. That which looked perfect to Lot's natural eyes became the downfall of his family. He found himself in a city given over to sexual immorality and under the impending judgment of God. Subsequently, he fled for his life while fire and sulfur rained down on Sodom and Gomorrah, losing his wife and possessions in the process. Later, his own daughters made him drunk and defiled him. This particular account illustrates that when attempting to make godly decisions, one simply cannot judge a book by its cover. We see time and again in the course of the biblical narrative that in order to walk in faith, we must not depend on our natural sight. Rather than making our decisions based solely on external appearances, we need to develop our spiritual senses so we can discern where the place of greatest blessing lies.

Boston, Massachusetts, has been my home since 1998 and it is my favorite city in the world. However, since taking up residence here, a continual procession of people have attempted to explain to me why Boston is not the most reasonable place to live. These reasons do not lack substance – the price of living is high, the winters are frigid, the spiritual atmosphere is difficult, the people are rude, etc. In spite of all these objections, however, Boston is the ideal location for my family for one undeniable reason: God has told us to call it home. Through this promise, we have confidence that we are sitting on a gold mine of His grace. We are perfectly positioned for what God wants to do in our lives, in our neighbors and in the nations of the earth.

Several years after our church planting team moved to Boston, a woman on our oversight team had a prophetic word of encouragement from Scripture that read:

> *This is what the LORD Almighty, the God of Israel, says to all those I carried into exile from Jerusalem to Babylon: "Build houses and settle down; plant gardens and eat what*

they produce. Marry and have sons and daughters; find wives for your sons and give your daughters in marriage, so that they too may have sons and daughters. Increase in number there; do not decrease. Also, seek the peace and prosperity of the city to which I have carried you into exile. Pray to the LORD for it, because if it prospers, you too will prosper." (Jeremiah 29:4-7)

As she conveyed this scripture to us, our spirits were greatly strengthened. We understood that the Lord was directing us not to simply "pass through" Boston, but to put down roots in this difficult spiritual environment and expect it to become a land of fruitfulness. Jeremiah spoke in the preceding passage to those from Judah who had recently been exiled to Babylon. They were not living in Judah, their beloved homeland, and longed to return. Nevertheless, the Lord gave them this command to encourage them not to waste their time in exile, but to seize the opportunity afforded them to influence the nation where they had been banished. As a result of living wholeheartedly in that place, those among whom the Israelites lived would receive the blessing of God.

By fully giving ourselves to God's purposes where we currently live and work, God will be faithful to lead us based on that place of rest. Satan is a schemer who will attempt to deceive us into being half-hearted about our life and work. We should guard against a "doing time" mentality, waiting until we get to another place or position that seems more appealing. If we are not careful to fight against dissatisfaction, we may arrive at the new situation we coveted and discover that discontentment quickly returns. When we, like Abraham, see with God's eyes and listen to His voice, He enables us to stand firm and flourish in the land He has told us to live in.

CHAPTER 4

GOD'S FRIEND

What distinguished Abraham from so many people of his day was not his moral perfection, but that he lived as a friend of God. On the way to the Promised Land, he and Sarah stayed in Gerar where he shaded the truth while speaking with Abimilech the King (Genesis 20). Succumbing to fear, Abraham claimed that Sarah was his sister (she was actually his half-sister), but neglected to divulge the more pertinent detail that she was also his wife. Abimilech, seeing that Sarah was beautiful, took her for himself. God intervened, however, and did not allow the King of Gerar to violate Sarah. Divine protection was afforded Abraham even though he still had much to learn about trust and faith. God was not good to Abraham because Abraham was good; God was good to Abraham because God was good. He was devoted to Abraham in spite of the patriarch's weakness and transformed him through unconditional love to prepare him for greater tests of faith.

Take Your Son, Your Only Son

God knows what is most precious to us, and sooner or later He will challenge its place on the throne of our hearts. Abraham had received an oath from God Almighty that a son from his own body would eventually become a people as numerous as the sand on the seashore. He and his wife Sarah endured many long years while anticipating the unfolding of this promise. As time marched on and no child appeared, they felt compelled to question whether God's promise would ever be realized. The wait was much longer than they could have anticipated. Abraham was 100 years old and Sarah 90 by the time of Isaac's birth, the fulfillment of the promise. The name Isaac appropriately means "laughter." While they felt the sheer joy of having a child at such a late age, it also struck them as ridiculous. God delighted to carry things beyond their ability so He alone would receive the glory.

Before Abraham was able to see God's promise unfold, he had to face the ultimate test to determine what was truly on the throne of his heart. He was taken to the very limit of his faith. God foreshadowed what would happen to His very own Son when He told Abraham, *"Take your son, your only son, Isaac, whom you love, and go to the region of Moriah. Sacrifice him there as a burnt offering on one of the mountains I will tell you about"* (Genesis 22:2). In this severe mercy[3], God commanded Abraham to sacrifice his most precious possession, the son of the promise, at the top of a lonely mountain. The command completely defied logic and appeared to be a mistake of epic proportions. This decisive test for Abraham would determine whether he would obey God or make an idol of his long-awaited heir. God challenged Abraham's reasoning in order to reveal his heart and find out who held his true allegiance.

In his book *Spiritual Authority* Watchman Nee explains, "The earthly life of the Lord Jesus was entirely above reason. What reason could there be for the disgrace, the lashing, and the crucifixion which he suffered? But he submitted himself to God's authority; He neither argued nor questioned; He only obeyed!"[4] The most valued possessions that we have tend to rule our lives without a violent surrender of them before the throne of God. Abraham followed through with this excruciating relinquishment and became the father of our faith. When his son Isaac inquired concerning the sacrifice, Abraham boldly pronounced, *"God himself will provide the lamb for the burnt offering, my son"* (Genesis 22:8). Abraham ascended to the top of the mount fully convinced that God had the power to raise his son from the dead. After building an altar and binding his son, Abraham took the knife to slay Isaac. Only after his complete obedience did God provide a ram to spare Abraham's son from death. From this point forward, God was not merely known as *Elohim,* "the Mighty" or "Very Great" divine being, but as *Jireh*, our "Provider."

This was a critical juncture for the spiritual father of faith. Obedience was not optional for Abraham, but was an essential element of his spiritual growth. To those who, like him, are ruthless in obedience, God is endless in his spiritual supply. As Hudson Taylor, missionary to China and founder of the China Inland Mission proclaimed, "God's work, done God's way, will never lack God's supplies."[5]

If we lack a thorough understanding of God's nature, we will be hindered in our obedience to Him. God enabled Abraham to overcome the trial of a lifetime because he passed a series of smaller tests along the way. God had proven Himself trustworthy to our spiritual father throughout the course of his life. Though he was a man who had emotions similar to ours, he learned through godly instruction not to be ruled by them. When we face a crossroad in our own lives, it is good to understand what role emotions are playing in our decision making process. Similarly, we should determine whether the spirit of fear or the confidence of faith is operating as the guide.

The deepest question in the heart of a man is not primarily where to go (locational) or what to do (vocational), but *who to trust*. Each person must decide whether God can be trusted to lead. When we cling to fear and human reasoning we crimp the endless supply of grace that could be readily available. Dean Sherman of Youth With a Mission describes Satan's voice as the roar of a lion (1 Peter 5:8). One of the reasons that the "king of the jungle" roars is in order to incite fear so he can capture and kill his prey. In the spiritual realm, Satan roars through fear, lust, rejection, and a host of other emotions in order to control our actions. Many of our major decisions in life can be based solely on emotion alone. As new creations in Christ, however, we have power from God to choose not to be led by negative emotions.[6] Let us not act without the peaceful assurance of His voice, and when we hear it, we must let no unholy emotion stop us from the prize of an obedient life.

God's Friend

The Apostle James declared:

> Was not our ancestor Abraham considered
> righteous for what he did when he offered his
> son Isaac on the altar? You see that his faith
> and his actions were working together, and his
> faith was made complete by what he did. And
> the scripture was fulfilled that says,
> "Abraham believed God, and it was credited
> to him as righteousness," and he was called
> God's friend. (James 2:21-23)

God created mankind to share friendship with Him, and
He has longed for that companionship to be restored ever since
the fall of man. He is not looking for someone to simply
follow a set of rules and regulations, or one that is content with
God at a distance. His heart desires a companion, one He can
truly call a friend. God found this kind of relationship with
Abraham. This simple man was someone with whom God
could share His heart. He was one who would walk with God
and talk with Him; laugh with Him and cry with Him. God
found in Abraham a true friend who walked by faith, and it
pleased Him very much. The writer of Hebrews states,
"without faith it is impossible to please God" (Hebrews 11:6).
If we wish to please God as Abraham did, we will listen for
His "still, small voice" (1 Kings 19:12). We will go when He
says to go. We will surrender every possession to God to be
found pleasing to Him, not necessarily perfect in our response,
but willing to risk everything for the God who is unseen. It
will not always be an easy course, for it is a narrow way.
Though the way with Him is narrow, difficult, and less
traveled, it is with Him; and that compensation makes the
journey well worth it.

SECTION 3

JOSEPH - I WILL NEVER LEAVE THEE

*Our circumstances are not an accurate reflection of
God's goodness. Whether life is good or bad, God's
goodness, rooted in His character, is the same.
- Helen Grace Lescheid, Author of "Lead, Kindly Light"*

The longest narrative in the Pentateuch relates the testimony of Joseph, far exceeding in length the stories of Abraham, Isaac or Jacob. There is much to be learned by delving into the biography of this impressive biblical figure. Countless times as I have read through the account of Joseph and observed his patience, humility and commitment to holiness, it has issued a rebuke to the selfish ambition, impatience and licentiousness in my own life. His path was full of hardship and temptation, but Joseph experienced God as the Faithful One who never left him, no matter how it may have appeared at the time.

While on a mission trip to New Orleans, Louisiana, in 1990, our church's discipleship training school stopped at a Wendy's restaurant for lunch. Young and zealous, we were filled with anticipation for all that God had in store for us. We shared the good news of Jesus with many of those who were working and eating in the restaurant and had the time of our lives. When we arrived at our van to continue on to New Orleans, someone noticed that a cassette tape was attached to our door handle. A note wrapped around it read, "I thought you might be blessed by listening to this." We were puzzled as to who would have known that this was our van since it was a rented vehicle. The cassette was entitled "I Will Never Leave Thee" and it was a message by a woman named Darlene Deibler Rose, who was as yet unknown to us. As we drove down the highway while listening, God's presence filled the van and we were all brought to tears by her testimony.

Darlene Rose was born in Boone, Iowa, and raised in a Christian home. At the age of ten she felt called to the mission field and was honored that God would even notice her. In her early twenties, she married and went to Indonesia as a missionary with her husband Russell shortly before World War II. Darlene told of the severe hardships that she endured, including the death of her husband in a prison camp of the Japanese Imperial Army and her own imprisonment amidst rats, rabies and the ravages of war. She was then moved to another prison camp where she spent time on death row after being falsely accused of spying. The guards regularly tortured her while her only sustenance was rice porridge filled with maggots. Malaria and severe dysentery were among the other hardships she suffered during that time. Darlene, who was an elderly woman at the time of this recording, spoke with poignancy about that season of her life. She explained, "Beloved, there were many times that I thought my Lord had left me during those years. However, I don't regret those years in the least; those were the best days of my life, because it was during those years that I learned the truth of what my Lord said, 'I will never leave thee nor forsake thee.'"[7] What a blow she struck to our modern sensual Christianity that equates God's blessing with ease and comfort! Darlene, like Joseph centuries earlier, found God to be an ever-present help in times of trouble (Psalm 46:1-GWT 1995).

CHAPTER 5

FROM A DREAM TO A DUNGEON

Joseph was his father's favorite son, receiving Jacob's love, affection and a multi-colored coat as a sign of honor. His brothers were already simmering with jealousy at the special treatment he had received before this gift, and resented the implied superiority. Then, Joseph had a dream, a promise from God that confirmed that his family would bow before him and give him honor (Genesis 37). This dream, though an assurance of future leadership, was not at all popular with his brothers. Whether maliciously or naively, he relayed this dream to his family causing his father to rebuke him saying, *"What is this dream you had? Will your mother and I and your brothers actually come and bow down to the ground before you?"* (Genesis 37:10). His brothers' jealousy came to a boiling point when Joseph went out to the fields to check on them and they threw him into a pit. They then sold him to a caravan of Midianites heading toward Egypt. Joseph's promise of leadership seemed to be going in the wrong direction, and he appeared to have been forsaken by his God.

The place between the promise of God and the fulfillment of that promise is often a test of our character as Christians. The question for Joseph in this time of difficulty was whether he would serve God when it seemed that he had been forgotten. God found in Joseph a man who would pass the test.

There is much to glean from looking at Joseph's response to the trials he endured. He understood that waiting on the Lord did not mean wasting his time. Joseph paid attention to those around him and did not miss the moment to serve. While he was in captivity at the house of Potiphar, Joseph refused to wallow in self-pity and was free of bitterness. The narrative continues, *"The LORD was with Joseph and he prospered, and he lived in the house of his Egyptian master. When his master saw that the LORD was with him and that the LORD gave him success in everything he did, Joseph found favor in his eyes and became his attendant"* (Genesis 39:2-3). Joseph's attitude and work ethic blessed Potiphar greatly and as a result everything was put under this Hebrew's command. In contrast to Joseph, many of us are tempted to wait until we find the right church, buy a new house, get married, or get the job promotion we desire before we consider giving our full attention to the Lord. But if we wait for these external things to get settled first, we may be waiting for the rest of our lives. God's will for us is to be wholehearted in devotion to Him in the present moment, and devoted to those He has placed in our immediate path. The Lord is able to move wholehearted people to godly action, while half-hearted people move only in response to their own impulses.

Joseph did not wait until everything worked out in his favor before he gave his full attention to God and man. He knew that divine eyes were observing how he responded to the unpleasant assignments that came his way. Only after proving himself faithful in these mundane things was God able to entrust Joseph with true responsibility. Based on this truth, we teach the leaders at our church not to resent the difficult person who comes to a small group meeting. God desires to see how young leaders love such a person before He gives them a new assignment. Godly leadership ability is not tested with the all-stars but with the outcasts. Our ability to love is not expanded as much with those who we gravitate toward as it is with those who test our patience.

Immediately following my graduation from Texas A&M University, I moved to Waco, Texas, to go through the Master's Commission training school based at Highland Baptist Church. After a few weeks in Waco, I became discouraged about my lack of connection with the other training school students. Though I sought God after surrendering to Jesus during my junior year at A&M, I still considered myself pretty "cool." The other Master's Commission students did not relate to my fraternity style and differed greatly from my college cohorts. They didn't appreciate my sense of humor, our social interactions were awkward at times, and I found my situation to be quite lonely. Crying out to God, I attempted to inform Him that something was very wrong with my current situation. He lovingly but firmly replied to my heart, "No Jeff, something is really right here. Until you learn to love those who are not similar to you, you haven't really learned how to love." This holy rebuke has given me perspective through the years and helped me expand my ability to love a wide range of people. We miss out on the beautiful diversity of the Body of Christ if we only stay within our own relational comfort zone. Joseph spent years in captivity serving those who were difficult to love, unaware that he was being prepared by God to shepherd an entire nation.

While at Potiphar's house, Joseph showed incredible strength of character and relentless trust in God. He had served his master admirably, but a major test of his integrity remained. Reeling from the recent rejection of his brothers, feeling lonely and vulnerable, an opportunity presented itself to Joseph to find comfort in an illicit relationship. His master's wife begged him to come to bed with her (Genesis 39:7). We should not suppose that this woman was unattractive to Joseph, especially when we consider the hormones that were raging within this teenager. The seduction emanating from her would have been enough to subdue a lesser man, but Joseph responded in a most God-fearing way and ran for his life. The scriptures explain:

> But he refused, "With me in charge," he told her, "my master does not concern himself with anything in the house; everything he owns he has entrusted to my care. No one is greater in this house than I am. My master has withheld nothing from me except you, because you are his wife. How then could I do such a wicked thing and sin against God?" And though she spoke to Joseph day after day, he refused to go

to bed with her or even be with her. (Genesis
39:8)

What an admirable man Joseph proved to be by refusing
her advances. Although self-pity and self-indulgence were
tempting options, he chose the godly way of escape. He
understood that the party who would be most offended by this
action was the Almighty God. By resisting temptation, he
honored the Lord and opened the floodgates of heavenly
mercy in an extraordinary way.

One would expect that Joseph would be immediately
honored for this act of spiritual heroism. Surely God would act
on his behalf and prove that sowing righteousness reaps a sure
reward. What actually came to pass was an altogether different
matter. Joseph was falsely accused by Potiphar's wife, framed
as a troublemaker, and received a stay in prison as his reward
(Genesis 39:19-20). Forgiving his brothers was an incredible
challenge, but dealing with the temptress was an altogether
different test: was he being humiliated and then punished for
obeying God?

"Karate Kid" (1984) is an inspiring movie that came out
during my senior year of high school. It contains a prime
illustration that God's preparatory work in our lives often
comes through what seem to be unrelated and pointless events.
In the movie, Daniel LaRusso is a teenage boy living in New
Jersey with his mother when a job transfer leads them to
California. After moving across the country, he attends high
school and is bullied by a boy named Johnny, who is the
ringleader of a group of thugs that belong to a karate school.
Coincidentally, Daniel finds out that the caretaker of his
apartment complex, Mr. Miyagi, is from Japan and an expert
in the art of karate. Miyagi agrees to take Daniel under his
wing and to teach him to defend himself. On the first day of
training, Daniel paints a fence, the next day he waxes Miyagi's
cars, and on the third day he sands a deck. Daniel's frustration
grows as he performs these menial jobs that have no apparent

connection to karate. After the conclusion of the third day, an aggravated Daniel approaches Mr. Miyagi with the complaint that his time has been completely wasted. Miyagi suddenly throws a punch at Daniel who is surprisingly able to deflect it. His teacher continues to come at him with punches and kicks, and Daniel is able to repel each one of them. The realization strikes Daniel that Mr. Miyagi has been teaching him karate all along through these seemingly unrelated assignments.

God often teaches us in the same way. He is preparing us for the battle ahead with exactly what we need for success and He can be trusted. Through what often seems meaningless, trivial, and of no consequence, He is training us to be victorious in our lives and enabling us to deliver others out of darkness. God wants us to be prepared, but He alone knows how to do it, and He alone can be trusted. True wisdom does not reside in understanding why God is doing what he is doing, but trusting Him in the midst of it. A desire to understand why everything has occurred is detrimental to our trust of God. We must take the attitude of the psalmist who says:

> *My heart is not proud, O LORD, my eyes are not haughty; I do not concern myself with great matters or things too wonderful for me. But I have stilled and quieted my soul; like a weaned child with its mother, like a weaned child is my soul within me.* (Psalm 131:1-2)

Joseph served God and men in the midst of his suffering and did not allow human reasoning to overcome his trust in the goodness of God.

In our relationship with the Lord, what often seems like cruelty in the moment becomes kindness for a lifetime. One of the most difficult trials a godly person can encounter is to feel abandoned by God after being obedient to Him. Faithful Joseph knew the big picture of God's promise of leadership, but the way he obtained that promise was completely different from what he could have ever imagined.

CHAPTER 6

BITTER OR BETTER

It is a delight to see how Joseph, this prince among his brothers, had a godly response to that which came his way. As we follow the course of events, we read:

> *Joseph's master took him and put him in prison, the place where the king's prisoners were confined. But while Joseph was there in the prison, the LORD was with Him; He showed him kindness and granted him favor in the eyes of the prison warden. So the warden put Joseph in charge of all those held in the prison, and he was made responsible for all that was done there. The warden paid no attention to anything under Joseph's care, because the Lord was with Joseph and gave him success in whatever he did.* (Genesis 39:20-23)

Even in prison, Joseph was entrusted with authority due to his integrity and unwavering trust in God. As a result, he was successful in whatever he undertook.

Joseph had passed many tests, but his time of trial had not yet drawn to a close. He correctly interpreted the dreams of Pharaoh's cupbearer and baker, his fellow prisoners, and pleaded with the cupbearer not to forget him after he was released from jail. The king's servant promised to mention Joseph's situation to Pharaoh when he was restored to his office. Two long years passed following the cupbearer's deliverance, yet he made no mention of Joseph to Pharaoh. Once again, Joseph seemed to have been overlooked by God. However, Pharaoh had a dream one day and no one was able to interpret it. The cupbearer remembered his oversight and mentioned Joseph to Pharaoh. God's preparatory work was finally complete and Joseph's day of promotion was at hand. When Joseph was brought out to interpret the dream, his humility was immediately evident. He not only interpreted Pharaoh's dream, but he acknowledged that it was not due to his own ability. A depth of understanding borne from years of godly training enabled Joseph to correctly assess the impending crisis, but Joseph gave no hint of self-promotion. Instead, he pronounced, *"And now let Pharaoh look for a discerning and wise man and put him in charge of the land of Egypt"* (Genesis 41:33). Pharaoh was so impressed with the man standing before him that he declared, *"Since God has made all this known to you, there is no one so discerning and wise as you"* (Genesis 41:39). In one day, Joseph ascended to the second in command of the entire kingdom of Egypt. Joseph, through consistent obedience in times of darkness, allowed God to be his promoter.

Whenever I feel overlooked, God reminds me that He will promote those who are wholly His, and only He knows the right time for this to happen. He is sovereign over the affairs of men and can be trusted even when the promise seems distant. As the Psalmist proclaimed, *"I was young and now I am old, yet I have never seen the righteous forsaken or their children begging bread"* (Psalm 37:25). When we serve God with whole hearts as Joseph did, not wasting time, but waiting expectantly with lives full of love and service, He will prove Himself, as always, faithful.

Lord of the Process

During a Vineyard Conference in Anaheim, California, in the mid 1980s, a woman gave a powerful testimony the day after she was healed. She had suffered from a paralyzing disease following her conversion to Christ that left her in a wheelchair.[8] With legs atrophied from lack of use, she stood next to the wheelchair that had held her the night before and spoke of God's miraculous work in her life. Many people had prayed for her to be healed over the previous five years and she frequently asked, "How long am I going to wait before I am healed, Lord?" Yet, as she was being healed she found herself saying, "So soon, Lord?" This is a profound example of the feeling one has when receiving a long-awaited promise from God. That which felt unbearably slow while waiting on the promise proves to be incredibly brief when faith becomes sight.

God has prepared a wonderful future for those who trust Him. Through the prophet Jeremiah, the Lord spoke:

> *"For I know the plans I have for you,"*
> *declares the LORD, "plans to prosper you and*
> *not to harm you, plans to give you a hope and*
> *a future. Then you will call upon me and come*
> *and pray to me and I will listen to you. You*
> *will seek me and find me when you seek me*
> *with all your heart."* (Jeremiah 29:11-13)

God revealed to rebellious Israel the true desire of His heart, which was to prosper them and not to harm them. God was the initiator, and the people of Israel had a choice of whether or not they would follow His lead. We are faced with the same opportunity today as God's people. He has chosen us, but we must decide whether to respond to His divine promptings. He has pursued us, but we must run after Him as well. He desires His preferred future for us, but we must not allow ourselves to be disqualified from His plans by careless-ness or lack of obedience. Joseph determined to cling to God and His word, and as a result, he qualified for the purposes that God had planned for him. Let us respond to God when He calls our name, and let us seek Him through the darkest of times until we see the fulfillment of His holy promise.

Joseph was free of bitterness and full of life, displaying the truth that no one else can ruin your life. When his brothers came to obtain food for their families (Genesis 42), Joseph did test them, but in the end he gave glory to God for His divine providence. After their father Jacob died, Joseph's brothers were in great fear of retribution, but he tenderly spoke:

> *"Don't be afraid. Am I in the place of God? You intended to harm me, but God intended it for good to accomplish what is now being done, the saving of many lives. So then, don't be afraid. I will provide for you and your children." And he reassured them and spoke kindly to them.* (Genesis 50:19-21)

A number of years ago, I developed a friendship with a man named Mike whose story powerfully illustrates the overcoming spirit that marked Joseph's life. Mike was filled with such joy that his boisterous laugh was easily distinguishable in a room full of people. When I would hear an outburst of laughter from him during a church service, my spirit would be strengthened and joy would fill my heart. He was a living example of the fullness of life that God brings to one who trusts in Him.

Mike invited me to his home one evening for dinner. As we shared a meal, he relayed to me the powerful testimony of his life in God. He was a Jewish believer who had suffered alienation from his family for the sake of Christ. When he was a teenager, his parents disowned him because of his decision to follow Jesus, and they refused to communicate with him over the following two decades. One fateful night, after twenty years of daily prayer, Mike's father called him to his deathbed and he flew home immediately to be with his parents. He arrived at their house and later rejoiced as they both surrendered their lives to Jesus that very night. As Mike's journey unfolded, I stood in awe of the God who is able to bring beauty from ashes.

The story, however, was just beginning. Mike then revealed that he had been married a number of years earlier to the woman of his dreams. He shared the heart-wrenching details of her death at the hands of a drunk driver, which occurred only six weeks into their marriage. Stunned at this turn of events, my first question was, "How did this affect your relationship with the Lord?" He candidly explained that it was a very difficult season, and for a time he struggled with bitterness toward the Lord. Eventually, he chose to release the bitterness and accept what God had in store for his future. Though devastated at the loss of his wife, he began to appreciate the opportunities made available to him that would have been more difficult as a married man. He ministered to youth, received calls at all hours for counseling and encouragement, and had much time to give to those he was discipling. After he shared this victory, another question arose, "Mike, this is a wonderful testimony, but don't you ever get lonely?" He responded with a statement that has changed my perspective to this day. He simply said, "Yes, Jeff, I still get lonely at times, but when that happens, I try to think of someone lonelier and I give them a call." Here was a man, like Joseph, who refused to be embittered and defeated by the circumstances of life. The outcome of Mike's obedience to Jesus was a joyously sacrificial life that was pleasing to God.

God has ordained a magnificent destiny for His children. The path to that preferred future however, is often offensive to the natural mind. Through a study of Joseph's life, we come to realize that even when the path is unclear, God is still the Lord of the process. Joseph had a determination that no one else could ruin his life and that God could be trusted even when he felt completely forgotten. There are times in life when, like Joseph, that which we hoped for looks far away, and we seem to be going in the opposite direction of our destination in God. When all is said and done, however, God will be vindicated and His ways toward us will be proven to be what they have always been - perfect.

SECTION 4

MOSES – PATIENCE & PRESENCE

The race is not to the swift or to the strong,
but to those who keep on running.
- Author Unknown

Since the creation of mankind, the eyes of God have searched for a man who would carry out His will on earth and allow Him to display His goodness. The exiles in Babylon received a message from God through Ezekiel whereby God announced, *"I looked for a man among them who would build up the wall and stand before me in the gap on behalf of the land, so I would not destroy it, but I found none"* (Ezekiel 22:30). God's heart breaks when He cannot find a person to carry out His will. He is complete in grace, mercy and power, yet in His divine order there must be a conduit of His grace to accomplish His purposes on the earth.

Moses was God's man for Israel during the oppressive reign of the Egyptians. He was the appointed instrument for the deliverance of the Israelite slaves from their ruthless taskmasters, but many years transpired before he was ready to carry out the epic task for which he had been created.

As is true of so many people throughout the Biblical narrative, Moses' name carries prophetic significance. Pharaoh decreed that all Israelite baby boys be put to death (Exodus 1), so Moses' mother hid him for three months after his birth. She finally sent him down the Nile in a basket, where Pharaoh's daughter providentially discovered him. When the Egyptian princess saw the helpless child, her heart was full of pity, and she took him as her own. She named him Moses, literally meaning, "drawn out" or "delivered out of water." This name spoke of his prophetic destiny. He would later deliver the Israelites from their Egyptian captors through water (the Red Sea). But between the promise and the fulfillment thereof,

Moses was required to learn through bitter experience about the patience and humility needed for leading God's people to freedom.

CHAPTER 7

FROM MIGHTY PRINCE
TO HUMBLE DELIVERER

Prince of Egypt

Moses grew up as an adopted son of the most powerful man in the entire land of Egypt. He lived a life of wealth, prosperity and privilege. Stephen, the church's first martyr, described Moses' upbringing in this way:

> *At that time Moses was born, and he was no ordinary child. For three months he was cared for in his father's house. When he was placed outside, Pharaoh's daughter took him and brought him up as her own son. Moses was educated in all the wisdom of the Egyptians and was powerful in speech and action.* (Acts 7:20-22)

By the age of forty, Moses had become powerful in speech and action in an Egyptian palace. Learning to be God's man, however, would require an entirely different set of circumstances. He had much to discover about the contrast between God's ways and man's ways.

Like Egypt in its day, my home of Boston is known as a center for higher education. It is home to Harvard, arguably the most prestigious university in the nation, as well as many other world class institutions. However, after living in Boston for many years, I am more assured than ever that the wisdom of man, as coveted as it might be, is still foolishness in God's sight. His value system is altogether different from the system of the world with which we are accustomed. A godly life is not achieved in the mastery of facts, but in dependence upon God. It is not attained in merely gaining information, but in a continual transformation of heart. Many of us succeeded in school by repeating information that we learned, and we received good marks for this accomplishment. But the true test of godliness is not in having the right answers; it is in responding rightly to what God asks of us. In the "information age," it is common to hear about new things, but there is a difference between *hearing* and *hearkening*. To hear is to listen and to know about, to hearken is to obey. By applying God's word and not merely hearing, we are actually learning as God intended. Further in Exodus we read:

> *One day, after Moses had grown up, he went out to where his own people were and watched them at their hard labor. He saw an Egyptian beating a Hebrew, one of his own people. Glancing this way and that and seeing no one, he killed the Egyptian and hid him in the sand. The next day he went out and saw two Hebrews fighting. He asked the one in the wrong, "Why are you hitting your fellow Hebrew?" The man said, "Who made you ruler and judge over us? Are you thinking of killing me as you killed the Egyptian?" Then Moses was afraid and thought, "What I did must have become known." When Pharaoh heard of this, he tried to kill Moses, but Moses fled from Pharaoh and went to live in Midian, where he sat down by a well.* (Exodus 2:11-15)

Moses had education and position, but he did not yet have the spiritual power necessary to rescue God's people. He attempted to fight for his people, the Israelites, by using the training he had received in Pharaoh's court. But the school of Egypt had only prepared him to use human strength and wisdom; he still needed to learn the ways of God.

Man has a tendency to be impressed with things that do not impress God. Man is impressed with a higher education, while God is impressed with a humble heart. Man is impressed with fame and fortune, while God is impressed with generosity of spirit. Man is impressed with "bigger" and "more," while God is impressed with simplicity and purity. What a lesson Moses was to learn over the next forty years of his life!

Years in the Desert

Moses is portrayed in many movies, like the classic Cecil B. DeMille epic *The Ten Commandments* with Charlton Heston, and the animated *Prince of Egypt* by DreamWorks. Some of these movies depict Moses returning to Egypt to deliver God's message to Pharaoh as a robust forty-year old with amazing pectoral muscles and wavy brown hair. But in actuality, Moses was *eighty* years old before he returned from the *forty* years of God's dealings in the desert. Moses had learned vital lessons of patience and dependence on God while he was living in Midian. Moses learned how to be strong in the flesh while he was growing up in Egypt, but he learned to be strong in the Lord while spending forty years of suffering the pain and challenges of the desert.

While I was waiting in line for food a few years ago at an international conference for our mission's organization, Darrell Atwood, a father in the Lord of mine, spoke a scripture over me. Sensing my eagerness to get something to eat in the crowded food line, Darrell said in King James English, *"By patience possess ye your soul"* (Luke 21:19). Darrell was poking fun, but when a man who has walked with the Lord for over half a century speaks God's word, it has impact. The scripture that Darrell encouraged me with that day has stayed with me since, and has added to my personal arsenal in God, protecting my soul. In order to have true godly influence, we must learn to live with faith to raise the dead while retaining the ability to endure what seems to be mundane activity over long periods of time.

By the time Moses saw the burning bush in the wilderness after four decades of attending to the mundane (Exodus 3:2-4), he was a different man. Through years of obscurity, he had been emptied of self, and God had prepared him for such a great task. Through tending sheep in the desert, Moses was allowed to see God's heart for His people. The Israelites were as helpless and defenseless as little sheep and were in need of a great deliverance. The cry of the Israelites had reached God, and He was determined to set them free from their oppression in Egypt. God had found a man to co-labor with, a man who could be used as an instrument of His power. The Lord was willing, and now His man was ready; the appointed time had finally arrived.

Moses had learned his lesson on humility, but almost too well. When God spoke to him from the burning bush, Moses' initial response was, *"O LORD, please send someone else to do it"* (Exodus 4:13). Here was the great son of Pharaoh, learned in all of the ways of the Egyptians, finally broken before God. He was no longer confident in his own abilities, but his eyes were still on himself. Moses now needed a final divine encouragement to catapult him into his assignment in God. We read:

> *Then the Lord's anger burned against Moses and he said, "What about your brother, Aaron the Levite? I know he can speak well. He is already on his way to meet you, and his heart will be glad when he sees you. You shall speak to him and put words in his mouth; I will help both of you speak and will teach you what to do. He will speak to the people for you, and it will be as if he were your mouth and as if you were God to him. But take this staff in your*

hand so you can perform miraculous signs with it." (Exodus 4:14-17)

This dialogue between the Lord and Moses at the burning bush affirms that when God commands us to do the impossible, help is already on the way.

God-sized callings cannot be accomplished alone, but as we step out in faith, He will send us help to achieve the impossible in His name. Through our own obedience, God releases others into the will of God. Many believers are caught in spiritual logjams, because they are waiting until everything is just right before they will obey God. When God wants to change the status quo, He often calls someone to attempt that which seems to be unattainable. Man's work is accomplished in the possible realm, while divine work is accomplished in the impossible realm.

Much of the work in the Body of Christ in the Western world revolves around what is possible for humans to accomplish. Due to the fear of stepping out into the unknown, we attempt to ensure that everything is plausible and safe before we proceed. The church planting movement I belong to values taking risks to make Christ known. One way that we accomplish this is by continually going on mission trips to distant countries throughout the world. We are not attempting to be dangerous, just obedient to the command of Christ to make disciples of all nations. Many of the places to which we travel, though, seem to intimidate many God-loving, church-going people. Questions often arise regarding our safety, the financial cost, and the ever present needs at home. Though these are questions we should consider, they should never take precedence over the accomplishment of God's will on earth. When I helped lead a short-term team to Afghanistan in 1998, it seemed a foolish venture to the natural mind because the oppressive Taliban regime was ruling with an iron fist at that time. However, two of the team members on that particular trip, Dayna Curry and Heather Mercer, were called by God to live among the Afghan people and saw an amazing work on behalf of that nation, which is chronicled in their book, *Prisoners of Hope*.[9] By obedience, and in the face of opposition, a door was opened that allowed the glory of God to shine.

When we go to far-flung places in obedience to God, it can seem beyond our financial means as well. While preparing to go on mission trips with our training schools through the years, a student will invariably ask me what we will do if we do not have enough money. An answer that has come to me through the years is simple; "There is no plan B." God has always provided, and He always will. Money is not the issue in being able to accomplish the will of God in the nations; obedience is the key to seeing the world won to Christ. Having traveled to forty countries at this point in my life, I have had the precious opportunity to preach the gospel in many diverse places. God has proven time and again that He will provide when I obey.

Moses obeyed and God enabled him to lead a deliverance of unmatched proportions. From the moment Moses arrived back on the scene in Egypt, the power of God was evident through his life. The ten plagues were executed as judgment on the Egyptian oppressors through God's humble and obedient servant. Moses was now strong, as God intended. The Great Deliverer had a friend and partner in Moses through whom He could do the good He had intended for the nation of Israel. By the time the Israelites left the land of Egypt, their enemies were showering them with gifts for their journey. Although Pharaoh soon changed his mind about letting the Israelites go, the Lord did not. While the Israelites stood at the edge of the Red Sea with the armies of Egypt bearing down on them, we read, *"Moses answered the people, 'Do not be afraid. Stand firm and you will see the deliverance the LORD will bring you today. The Egyptians you see today you will never see again'"* (Exodus 14:13).

What God had decided was firm; His people were free. The Egyptian army was swallowed in the heart of the sea, while the Israelites passed through the water to safety on the other side. They rejoiced in their God and in their leader Moses, who together had wrought a great liberation that would be recounted for generations to come.

CHAPTER 8

MAY YOUR PRESENCE GO WITH US

The battle had been won, but the war was still raging for the destiny of Israel and their humble leader. God had set the Israelites free from those who oppressed them, but in order to inherit the Promised Land, they had to pass through the desert. Though they had experienced freedom from bondage, they were not yet mature. They needed to be open to the Lord's instruction and eager for His presence. Being teachable is a characteristic of all who move past childish ways and grow to maturity in their faith. We see this exhibited most profoundly in Moses' life when his father-in-law, Jethro, visited him in the desert (Exodus 18). After Moses recounted the Lord's faithfulness to the Israelites, Jethro observed him as he judged the people of Israel. Everyone came directly to Moses from morning to evening with their disputes and dilemmas. As Moses was judging the people, it would not be a stretch to imagine him thinking about how impressive this appeared. He was leading a vast people and having everyone approach him for a decision.

The Test of Teachability

If this was what Moses was pondering, he was in for a surprise. Jethro, instead of encouraging Moses with how proud he was of him, made this statement: *"What you are doing is not good. You and these people who come to you will only wear yourselves out. The work is too heavy for you; you cannot handle it alone. Listen now to me and I will give you some advice, and may God be with you"* (Exodus 18: 17-19). Consider that Jethro, the mere priest of Midian, was addressing Moses, the deliverer of all Israel. Had Moses been less humble, he could have laid out his extensive resume and resisted this godly rebuke. Moses, however, was a mature man who instead of getting defensive took his father-in-law's advice and immediately applied it by appointing leaders of 10s, 100s and 1000s. When he realized that there was a more effective way to lead the people, Moses was able to shift his paradigm, and as a result he became more effective in serving and shepherding God's people. Moses exhibited the humility that had been borne in him over the course of years in the desert. This attribute, as much as any he possessed, enabled Moses to have God's full authority rest on him. Teachable ones like Moses are most qualified to be leaders in the Body of Christ and will continue to grow in godly influence and effectiveness to the end of their days.

God is Great, God is Good

Moses was not merely content with leading God's people, however; he insisted that God's presence be with them as they went. Moses, while seeking God at the tent of meeting, implored:

> You have been telling me, "Lead these people," but you have not let me know whom you will send with me. You have said, "I know you by name and you have found favor with me." If you are pleased with me, teach me your ways so I may know you and continue to find favor with you. Remember that this nation is your people." The Lord replied, "My Presence will go with you, and I will give you rest." Then Moses said to him, "If your Presence does not go with us, do not send us up from here. How will anyone know that you are pleased with me and with your people unless you go with us? What else will distinguish me and your people from all the other people on the face of the earth? "
> (Exodus 33:12-16)

My dear friend Sean Richmond was in prayer one day a number of years ago, and God revealed to him one of the most important requirements for effective ministry. He spoke to Sean's heart and said, "Perform for Me and I will watch, call out to Me and I will come!" God does not need us to perform *for Him*, but God desires for us to perform great exploits *with Him*.

People have often commented about the vibrancy and power of community that they experience while interacting with our churches in Boston. A conviction that has grown in me through the years is that true community cannot be borne with community as the ultimate goal, but instead, with the presence of God as paramount. There is a distinguishing characteristic of God's people when Jesus is central that makes clear to observers and participants alike that this is much more than a social club. The church of Jesus Christ, calling out to Him, is like no other people on the face of the earth. The great thing about us is the One who is among us.

As Moses called out to God for his glory, the Lord revealed himself through His holy word. After God told Moses to present himself on Mount Sinai, we read:

> *Then the Lord came down in the cloud and stood there with him and proclaimed his name, the Lord. And he passed in front of Moses, proclaiming, "The Lord, the Lord, the compassionate and gracious God, slow to anger, abounding in love and faithfulness, maintaining love to thousands, and forgiving wickedness, rebellion and sin. Yet he does not leave the guilty unpunished; he punishes the children and their children for the sin of the fathers to the third and fourth generation."* (Exodus 34:5-7)

In this passage, it is remarkable that God declared His goodness before proclaiming His greatness. As humans, we love to show our power first, but God did not do that when He revealed Himself to Moses. God could have shown Himself first as powerful, strong, mighty, or a host of other attributes that would have been fitting, but the first descriptive that He used while revealing Himself to Moses was the word, "gracious." This makes clear to us that God uses His power for good. God's glory is seen in that, although He is great in power, He chooses to relate to us through His goodness. The psalmist affirms this by declaring, *"One thing God has spoken, two things have I heard: that you, O God, are strong, and that you, O Lord, are loving. Surely you will reward each person according to what he has done"* (Psalm 62:11-12). In order to mature in our relationship with God, we need to understand the dual truth that He is "God Most Immanent" and "God Most Intimate." It is not enough to know that God is great and "up there beyond us;" we must also know that He is good and "down here with us." These two aspects of God's character are vitally important for us to understand in increasing measure if we are to flourish in our relationship with God. In order to overcome in some personal trials, we must know primarily that God is great, and during other trials we must know primarily that God is good.

Jack Gaston, a friend of mine, lost his wife to breast cancer a number of years ago. Through this friend, I saw an example of a man who knew both of these aspects of God's character. Diane was a wonderful woman of God who lived a healthy lifestyle, had five children and no family history of cancer. We were shocked to learn that she was diagnosed with an aggressive form of breast cancer at merely 33 years of age. Jack and Diane began to seek God, believing for His miracle-working power to heal her body. They knew God as an intimate friend who had provided so wonderfully for their needs throughout their marriage. Only a couple of years prior, their son Tyler had been healed of a snakebite that occurred on their family farm. The testimony was so encouraging that it was featured on Christian Broadcasting Network's 700 Club program.

As they believed God for Diane's healing, Jack would fast, pray, and quote scriptures of God's healing power to combat the cancer. For months, they continued to believe with a steadfast faith as Diane's health went from bad to worse. This couple was a powerful example to many as they sought God with all of their hearts and minds. My friend, Dr. Michael Jahrmarkt, and I went to the airport in Dallas to pick up the Gastons as they flew home from Kentucky after all natural means had been exhausted for Diane's healing. We took Diane to Parkland hospital in Dallas where she was examined for what felt like fluid on her lungs, which was causing her to have labored breathing. Following the procedure and analysis, the doctor caring for her entered her room and gently alerted Diane that what she was experiencing was not fluid, but cancer, which had metastasized into her lungs. It was humbling to watch as Diane looked at Jack and asked him what they would do about this report. He replied, "Diane, we do what we have been doing all along. We believe." Jack immediately began quoting verse after verse over Diane and she finally said the words, "The fight has just begun!"

The doctors sent Jack and Diane back to their home in Gatesville, Texas, the following day, and Diane receded further. She was soon using 100% oxygen, a sign that her days were numbered. Dr. Jahrmarkt was living at the Gaston house during that period, and I received a phone call from him one early morning. I remember him saying, "Jeff, Diane is gone...She is in the other room on the recliner and the children do not know that she has died yet." I immediately got dressed, jumped into my car and headed the forty-five miles to Gatesville, arriving at the Gaston house not sure what to expect. The five children were around the breakfast table with Michael, and Jack was making breakfast for them. It became clear as I looked at them that the children did not yet know about their mother's death.

The course of the morning left me in awe. While Michael and I were sitting on the porch, Jack shared with their children that their mother had passed on to eternity. Our hearts broke as we heard weeping coming from inside the house. After a short time, Diane's parents arrived, and we went back inside the house. Jack explained that after telling the children about their mother's death, he and his seven-year old son Trey had faith to pray for Diane to be raised from the dead. He stated that if anyone had faith, they could come into the back room and pray with them for her to be raised up from her chair. The other children, Diane's parents, Michael and I filed back into the room and joined Jack and Trey as they prayed for Diane. It was the first time I had ever laid my hand on a cold body, but we all prayed fervently for Diane with faith that she would be raised from the dead. After a long while, Jack stopped and said, "It's over." We all stopped praying and knew that he was right; Diane had passed through death into life eternal. It is my firm belief that God's mighty power was poured out on earth the day we prayed for Diane. Diane was not healed, but I believe that somewhere in the world God's healing power was released, because someone exercised faith and chose to believe.

That evening, we sat with Jack and the children as they shared a family devotional and determined to follow Jesus with all of their hearts in the coming days. Later, at the funeral, there was not a dry eye in the house. Jack, grieving from the loss of his precious wife, walked up to the front of the church, and what he said that day has never left me. He spoke so clearly of the importance of knowing God's character in the midst of trial. Jack spoke steadily, "From the time that Diane was diagnosed with cancer, we believed that God would heal her. We fasted, we prayed, and we believed. Even after she died we had faith that she would be raised from the dead, but she wasn't. There are many questions that we have today;

some are okay to ask and some are not. But the most important question that needs to be answered today is, 'Will we still believe?' I will not stop believing God to be who He says He is.'" The presence of God in the room was palpable as we saw a man trust in God and refuse to let circumstances, even confusion and disappointment, steal his faith.

As Moses discovered the character of God and relied on it through decades of leading the Israelites in the wilderness, so Jack, thousands of years later, relied on the character of God, and as a result impacted many lives. May we continually walk in the understanding that God is great and that God is good. These two coexistent truths about God's nature will see us through the darkest of nights and shine on us in the brightest of days.

SECTION 5

JOSHUA - WHOLEHEARTED

Wherever you are - be all there. Live to the hilt every situation that you believe to be the will of God.
- Jim Elliot, Missionary martyr to Ecuador

In 2 Chronicles 16:9 we read, *"The eyes of the Lord move to and fro throughout the earth that he may strongly support those whose heart is completely his"* (NASB). A heart wholly devoted to God is the one distinguishing characteristic above all others that sets Joshua's life apart from those of his contemporaries. In a generation where our passions are so often diluted by an abundance of loves, Joshua shines brightly as a beacon to light our way. He remained faithful to God and completed the assignment given to him by living with wholehearted devotion. As we look at Joshua's life, may we be inspired to live "to the hilt" for God.

CHAPTER 9

DISCIPLES ARE MADE, NOT BORN

The Value of a Spiritual Mentor

Joshua is a fitting name for the man whom God called to lead his people across the Jordan River and into the Promised Land. The name Joshua, which means, "Yahweh is Salvation," is the equivalent of the Greek name Jesus. God fulfilled his promise to Israel through Joshua and brought them into the "land of milk and honey." This is an accurate foreshadowing of what Jesus accomplished at the cross, where he delivered his people from the bondage of sin through His blood and ushered them into the promised inheritance of eternal life. Careful preparation is required for those who lead others to greatness, and Joshua was no exception. He went through an intense spiritual boot camp with a strong and loving drill sergeant, Moses. No one was better equipped to train Joshua than his predecessor, who was the most humble man on earth at the time. The Scripture states, *"Now Moses was a very humble man, more humble than anyone else on the face of the earth"* (Numbers 12:3). We would be hard-pressed to overestimate the profound influence that Moses, Joshua's mentor in righteousness, had upon this future leader of Israel.

Joshua must have marveled at Moses' faith when God delivered Israel and destroyed the Egyptian hordes in the Red Sea. He observed Moses parting the waters before the nation of Israel, modeling for Joshua what he would be called to accomplish some forty years later. We first see Joshua in Exodus 17 as he led the army of Israel in battle against the Amalekites. Moses had ordered him to fight while praying with Aaron and Hur on top of the mountain that overlooked the battle. Joshua defeated the Amalakites with the sword and won a great victory for Israel while Moses, held up by his companions, interceded for God's help. Moses could have fought this battle himself, but he understood that it was more important for Israel's future that Joshua learn through personal experience. Moses equipped Israel's future leader by entrusting him with ever-increasing responsibility, and then praying for him to succeed. He knew that the most important spiritual lessons are learned by doing, not merely by observing. Moses released Joshua into ministry and taught him through this experience of war. He operated with prophetic insight as he trained God's man of the future. If Moses had won the battle himself, with Joshua looking on or even helping, Joshua would not have been prepared for the greater battles ahead. Moses had won his battles, and now it was Joshua's time to lead while his mentor was still able to train him.

While Joshua was returning with Moses from the Mountain of God after Moses had received the Ten Commandments (Exodus 32), the opportunity presented itself for Moses to teach Joshua an important lesson in spiritual discernment. The Jews had reverted to pagan revelry while Moses was away, and the uproar from their camp could be heard from far away. While traveling down the mount, Joshua erroneously perceived it as a war cry. Seasoned from years of leadership, Moses corrected Joshua saying, *"It is not the sound of victory, it is not the sound of defeat; it is the sound of singing that I hear"* (Exodus 32:18). Moses was continually teaching his young charge as they shared their lives together. Joshua was eventually able to possess the Promised Land because he was committed to learning God's lessons and had submitted to Moses' leadership.

Bill Johnson, Senior Pastor of Bethel Church in Redding, CA, explains that King David mentored the only men in the Bible recorded to have killed giants. He concludes with this observation, "If you want to kill giants, hang around a giant killer."[10] We should partner with those who have great faith and godly character that expands our ability to be effective in God's kingdom. How grateful I am for the spiritual mentors with whom I have been associated. These men have taught me God's ways and demonstrated what it truly means to live wholeheartedly. Jimmy Seibert, my leader and friend, taught me to seek the Lord with all of my heart, and to live what I believe with fervency and consistency. Mark Buckner, another dear friend and mentor, believed in me while I was young, treated me with respect, and taught me what it means to dream the dreams of God. Without these men, and many others along the way, I would not have been fully prepared to walk the road less traveled.

Those who are not submitted to godly leadership miss out on the riches of this blessing, and their own leadership suffers as a result. If we refuse to learn from those who have gone before, others will be hindered from following us. Ruthless trust in God through submission to those of trustworthy character has been a source of true riches in my life. Blind spots are precisely that - the parts of us that we cannot see. Those in leadership over me have been faithful to point out these areas in my life and to bring the loving correction that is so good for my soul. Suzette Hattingh, a gifted teacher and prayer warrior, states it well: "Submission is protection and not restriction."[11] Joshua lived a life unhindered because he was fully submitted to God through human leadership.

Training for Righteousness

Joshua was a warrior who fought and won the battles of the Lord. His strength came from the quality of relationship that he had with God. Scripture states:

> *Now Moses used to take a tent and pitch it outside the camp some distance away, calling it the 'tent of meeting.' Anyone inquiring of the LORD would go to the tent of meeting outside the camp. And whenever Moses went out to the tent, all the people rose and stood at*

*the entrances to their tents, watching Moses
until he entered the tent. As Moses went into
the tent, the pillar of cloud would come down
and stay at the entrance, while the LORD
spoke with Moses. Whenever the people saw
the pillar of cloud standing at the entrance to
the tent, they all stood and worshiped, each at
the entrance to his tent. The LORD would
speak to Moses face to face, as a man speaks
with his friend. Then Moses would return to
the camp, but his young aide Joshua son of
Nun did not leave the tent.* (Exodus 33:8-11)

Moses went regularly to seek God regarding the Israelites.
After speaking with the Lord, he returned to the camp, but
Joshua stayed in the tent of meeting. He was not content with
just a taste of God; he was a man who was filled with an insati-
able desire to be in the divine presence of God. Joshua
diligently pursued God, and in those times he became familiar
with God's voice. His ability to hear God and obey would lead
him to the conquest of the Promised Land. Joshua was wholehearted in his relationship with the Lord and had a deep
revelation of God's character. He was a spiritual champion.

Champions must give their all in order to take home the
prize. They cannot merely dabble in their profession, nor play
at it from time to time only when they feel like practicing.
They must train and work when others are goofing around, and
their entire being must be given to the cause of victory. We
can observe this by looking at professional athletes or
musicians. In order to be the best, they make a decision to do
whatever it takes to succeed. Chris Carmichael, founder of
Carmichael Training Systems, says of Lance Armstrong, the
seven-time winner of the Tour de France:

Well, Lance trains more than his competitors.
He was the first to go out and actually ride the

important Tour stages in advance. He doesn't just wake up in July and say, '[Gosh], I hope I am ready for this race'. He knows he is ready, because he has whipped himself all year long. Armstrong describes his bike as his office. 'It's my job,' he told me. 'I love it, and I wouldn't ride if I didn't. But it's incredibly hard work, full of sacrifices. And you have to be able to go out there every single day.' In the morning, he rises, eats, and gets on his bike; sometimes, before a particularly long day, he waits to eat again (in order to store up carbohydrates) before taking off. We schedule his daily workouts to leave late in the morning, so that he can ride for six hours. He returns home about five or six o'clock, in time for a quick dinner—a protein-carb smoothie, a little pasta. Then it is time for bed.[12]

If this training is necessary for Lance Armstrong to pursue a temporal prize, how much more is this type of effort necessary for us who desire to be champions in our spiritual lives? Paul, addressing the undisciplined Corinthians, implored, *"Do you not know that in a race all the runners run, but only one gets the prize? Run in such a way as to get the prize"* (1 Corinthians 9:24). Joshua was "disciplined for godliness" (1 Timothy 4:8) and was not casual about God. He met the Lord in a real way that saturated him with divine presence. The Body of Christ lacks spiritual power when people are not committed to training for godliness. Speaking of the nation of Israel, the prophet Hosea states, *"Foreigners sap his strength, but he does not realize it"* (Hosea 7:9). When we are lazy about our approach to the things of God and do not commit to God as our source of life, our spiritual strength is sapped and we often do not even realize it. Joshua had spiritual power because he trained every day for righteousness. He was ready for the battle because he had put in the spiritual work beforehand.

CHAPTER 10

FAITH, POSSESSING GOD'S PROMISE

Faith, the Currency of Heaven

We must have faith in order to transact business in the kingdom of God. No matter how long we pray or how much we serve, if we lack faith, we will not be able to please God (Hebrews 11:6). Faith is sometimes described with the acronym "Forsaking All, I Trust in Him." Joshua knew that his home was in heaven, and he was able to see with spiritual eyes. As a young man, (Numbers 13), he was sent on an exploratory trip with a group of twelve men from the twelve tribes of Israel. Moses commanded them to observe and bring back a report concerning the people and terrain of the Promised Land. After their return, Joshua and Caleb proved to be men with a different, wholehearted spirit. While the rest of the spies brought back a fearful and faithless report, this holy pair was brimming with hope. Caleb proclaimed, *"We should go up and take possession of the land, for we can certainly do it"* (Numbers 13:30). The Lord saw that these two men had faith to transact holy business for his glory. Joshua possessed the spiritual riches to lead the people of Israel into the Promised Land.

C.T. Studd was a nineteenth century missionary pioneer to China, India and finally, the very heart of Africa. He had forsaken wealth and prestige as the best cricketer in England in the late 1800s and spent his life for Christ on the mission field. After serving in China for ten years and in India for six years, he received another call from God to go to Africa. He had suffered from asthma for many years, sleeping only from two to four in the morning while sitting in a chair, fighting for breath. This did not deter him, however. At the age of 52, C.T. wrote in regards to going to the unreached peoples of Africa:

We *should* go crusading for Christ...We
shout, 'onward Christian soldiers, marching
on to war,' and then?...and then?... we whis-
per, 'I pray Thee have me excused!!!' What
glorious humbugs we are...the heart of Asia,
the heart of Africa and well nigh the whole
continent of South America are untouched
with the Gospel of Christ. Last June, at the
mouth of the Congo there awaited a thousand
prospectors, traders, merchants and gold-
seekers, waiting to rush into these regions as
soon as the government opened the door to
them, for rumor declared that there is an
abundance of gold. If such men hear so loudly
the call of gold and obey it, can it be that the
ears of Christ's soldiers are deaf to the call of
God and the cries of the dying souls of men?
Are gamblers for gold so many and gamblers
for God so few?[13]

We must have the heart of Joshua, the zeal of Caleb, and
the hunger of C.T. Studd in order to complete the will of God
in our generation.

Possessing the Land

Moses was forbidden to enter the Promised Land and died
as result of his disobedient act in the Desert of Zin (Numbers
20:11). Joshua was prepared, and the time had arrived for the
promise to be fulfilled. God spoke to Joshua and said:

*No one will be able to stand up against you all
the days of your life. As I was with Moses, so I
will be with you: I will never leave you, nor
forsake you. Be strong and courageous, because you will lead these people to inherit the*

land I swore to their forefathers to give them.
(Joshua 1:5)

Joshua was not merely carrying out an order, but he was carrying with him the presence and the promise of God. He was following in the footsteps of the men who, like Moses, had received God's promise and acted in faith. Each of the Patriarchs - Abraham, Isaac and Jacob - received his own visitation from God, not relying on what God had said to his predecessor. He gave each of them the same promise: an inheritance of land and a blessing for all peoples on the earth through his offspring. Abraham told Isaac of the promise of God and Isaac to Jacob, but that was not sufficient. God revealed himself to each of these three men because He was not simply passing on information; He was giving each one His presence. Likewise, Moses and Joshua each received His presence alongside His promises.

Maturity in our faith is developed when we determine to pursue God above all other pleasures, calling out to Him for direct revelation and listening attentively for His voice. God desires to communicate with us *"face to face,"* but far too often, we believers in Christ are comfortable getting our revelation from God second-hand, hoping for someone else to hear God on our behalf. However, if received second-hand, it is only information. Revelation comes through a first hand encounter with God.

While leading a church planting team in Irkutsk, Siberia in the summer of 1993, I was desperate for such an encounter with God. I knew that what God had called me to do in that city was impossible in my own strength, and I recognized my need for Him in a fresh way. Each morning I arose early and walked along the Angara River near my apartment, seeking God's face with all my heart. Our team also sought Him daily with an intensity of purpose. His presence during that summer was as tangible to me as I had ever known, and out of that intimacy our team was able to see a church planting work begun in a distant land that has continued to this day. That experience provided me with a new insight: God takes us far from our home, "our place of comfort", to draw us near to His heart.

God's promise of His presence to Joshua was immediately followed by a crucial challenge:

> *Do not let this Book of the Law depart from your mouth; meditate on it day and night, so that you may be careful to do everything written in it. Then you will be prosperous and successful. Have I not commanded you? Be strong and courageous. Do not be terrified; do not be discouraged, for the LORD your God will be with you wherever you go.* (Joshua 1:8-9)

This command to Joshua is vital for all who wish to grow to full maturity in the Lord. We must meditate on the word of God continually in order to prosper in God's calling upon our lives.

Cliffs Notes was a true companion of mine in high school and college. These notes were my favorite study partner when I took a test on a book that I had not fully read. Though this is not the stated intent of these booklets, I used them in this way to help me complete my education. There is no shortcut, however, when it comes to being a student of the Bible. My faith consists of a strong belief in the present day working of the Holy Spirit and His power to do signs, wonders and miracles. However, after the "fire of God's power" falls upon someone, only the daily "washing" of the Word of God - that is, consistent time in the Scriptures ensures that the work of the Spirit will persist. The Spirit of God and the Word of God are inseparably linked. While the Spirit breaks the yoke of sin, the truth of Scripture will keep us free for the long term. Jesus revealed this truth while speaking with the woman at the well, saying, *"Yet a time is coming and has now come when the true worshipers will worship the Father in spirit and truth, for they are the kind of worshipers the Father seeks. God is spirit and His worshipers must worship in spirit and in truth"* (John 4:23-24).

The importance of the Word of God in our lives cannot be overestimated. Our minds should be renewed by God's word (Romans 12:2) in three key areas of truth. The first truth is about God's nature; His love and His power. We must have an ever-increasing understanding of the One we know and serve because the answer to life is in Him, not us. A second truth that is vital as we come to God's word is about who we are in Christ. It is fundamental that we realize our identity as a new creation, free from the power of sin and joyfully devoted as servants of righteousness. The final essential truth regards the nature of our enemy, the devil. We frequently forget that we are at war with an adversary whose devious and subtle tactics attempt to keep us from abundant life and effective ministry. Our gaze should be fixed upon God, but we must also be aware of the enemy and his schemes.

Many years ago, I was struggling with a particular sin pattern that seemed to cling to me and would not release its grip. A question entered my mind after repeated failure in this area, "Am I destined to be in this pattern for the rest of my life?" The answer that came to my heart was that the word of God would provide my deliverance. Night after night, I meditated on many verses in Romans 5 through 7 and committed myself to God. The CD player in my room was on repeat through the night as I listened to the Bible and trusted that it would sink into my subconscious. I clung to Jesus' promise, *"If you hold to my teaching, you are really my disciples. Then you will know the truth, and the truth will set you free"* (John 8:32). As I pursued accountability with friends, stayed in God's word and refused to surrender, over the course of time, the sin that held me for so long no longer had rule in my life. Likewise, Joshua, through seeking God in His word, "not letting it depart" (Joshua 1:8-NASB), would ensure freedom for himself and victory for those he led.

It is Satan's express intention that we compromise and make a truce with sin in our lives because it will steal our joy and hinder our effectiveness for God's kingdom. We ought never to give up in this battle against sin. It is necessary that we hold on to the truth until our deliverance is complete. Just as Hitler deceived those who made a truce with him prior to World War II, Satan will not keep his end of the bargain. He will not leave us alone until he knows that we will not surrender. Freedom from sin is completely possible, provided that we desire purity strongly enough.

By following God's word, Joshua obtained personal freedom and led the Israelites in a campaign to possess the inheritance that God delighted to give them. From the fall of Jericho (Joshua 6) to the defeat of the Anakites (Joshua 11), Joshua was victorious in all he undertook. He defeated a total of 31 kings, and we read, *"So Joshua took the entire land, just as the LORD had directed Moses, and he gave it as an inheritance to Israel according to their tribal divisions. Then the land had rest from war"* (Joshua 11:23). Joshua developed intimacy with God in the desert, learned invaluable lessons from his spiritual father, Moses, and stayed true to God's word throughout his lifetime. As a result, God was exalted and His people found rest. Joshua had lived up to his name; through him Yahweh became salvation for the people of God.

SECTION 6

SAMUEL – INTEGRITY

The best measure of a spiritual life
is not its ecstasies but its obedience.
- Oswald Chambers

Having a child had proved impossible for Hannah - praise God for miracles! Samuel's mother was unable to conceive and was taunted constantly by Peneniah, a rival wife who had already borne several children to their mutual husband El-kanah. No matter how much Elkanah tried to encourage her, Hannah was inconsolable. With great bitterness of soul, Hannah cried out to God at the house of the Lord in Shiloh. Assured by a word from Eli the priest, God granted Hannah's request and gave her a son, Samuel. She committed him to God for the rest of his life, and, after she weaned him, made good on her promise and brought Samuel to live at the house of the Lord with the high priest, Eli.

We read, *"The boy Samuel grew up in the presence of the LORD"* (1 Samuel 2:21). God's people were emerging from a dark four hundred year period where *"everyone did what was right in his own eyes"* (Judges 21:25), and *"the word of the LORD was extremely rare"* (1 Samuel 3:1). Samuel was a transitional figure who brought Israel out of the era of the judges and anointed the first two kings of Israel. The time was ripe for God to restore His people and bring them back under His protection. The Almighty desired to bring spiritual renewal, and He found the right man to accomplish His purpose.

Samuel is a complete contrast to the spiritual leaders of his day. He was a man of prophetic insight, of uncompromising integrity, and one who was instrumental in bringing the fear of God back to the people of Israel. By emulating his relationship with God and men, we can be a part of promoting renewal in our day.

CHAPTER 11

A LIFE OF SPIRITUAL IMPACT

Obeying God's Voice, Speaking God's Words

Samuel lived in the temple with Eli from his boyhood, and it was during this time that he learned to hear God's voice. A spiritually mature person has the ability to hear and to discern what God is saying on a continual basis. Samuel began this learning process at a very young age, while he was laying down to sleep one night in the house of God (1 Samuel 3:3). Three times he heard a voice say to him, "Samuel!" and each time he went to Eli, believing that the priest was calling him. The account continues, *"Then Eli realized that the LORD was calling the boy. So Eli told Samuel, 'Go and lie down, and if he calls you, say, 'Speak LORD, for your servant is listening"* (1 Samuel 3:8b-9). God called him once again, and this time Samuel responded as Eli had instructed him. The Lord spoke a strong prophecy against the house of Eli regarding his sons' blatant disobedience and Eli's failure to restrain them. Though unsettling to the young boy, it was a powerful initiation into learning to hear God's voice.

Hearing the audible voice of God must have been a powerful experience for Samuel, but he also needed to learn to hear God's voice through human authority. This required a greater measure of humility. Eli did not inspire confidence; he was old, overweight, and not sensitive to God's voice while Samuel was living in the temple. He was, however, the high priest of Israel and had been given authority in Samuel's life to instruct him. Samuel learned to hear God through first listening to his spiritual authority, Eli. When we unfairly judge those whom God places over us, we can miss clear direction from God. Those who are given spiritual authority in our lives are to be honored, regardless of their own weaknesses. The independent spirit that has pervaded the Body of Christ in recent decades must be forcefully resisted so that we are in a safe place to discern the voice of the Lord. Eli's sons partook of this spirit of independence and did not heed their father's rebuke (1 Samuel 2:25). As a result, they were struck down on the battlefield by God's righteous anger. Likewise, those who refuse to submit themselves to God-ordained spiritual authority will become slaves to disobedience and ultimately destroyed for their lack of knowledge (Hosea 4:6).

Because Samuel learned to hear and obey God's voice, he was empowered to be God's spokesman. God's word must come to us and must be worked into us in order for it to flow through us in power. We can repeat what others have said, but we will only have life-changing power when we speak from the crucible of personal experience. Francis Frangipane states, "Victory begins with the name of Jesus on our lips, but it is not consummated until the nature of Jesus is in our hearts."[14] Two people can speak about the same subject, but only the obedient one speaks with the power to change people's lives. The narrative continues:

> *The LORD was with Samuel as he grew up and he let none of his words fall to the ground. All Israel from Dan to Beersheba recognized that Samuel was attested as a prophet of the LORD. The LORD continued to appear at Shiloh, and there he revealed himself to Samuel through his word. And Samuel's word came to all Israel.* (1 Samuel 3:19-21)

This passage profoundly impacts me every time I read it. Samuel had no ineffective words; they all accomplished God's will. May the Lord deliver us from ineffective words and impotent lives. It is my continual prayer that the Lord would give me words and actions that change lives, a spiritual potency that has great effect. When we spend time listening to God's voice and taking risks to obey what He commands, we can be assured that our words will not "fall to the ground." They will have great impact and will even shake kings and kingdoms for His glory.

Agnes Gonxha Bojaxhiu, better known as Mother Teresa, was born in the Macedonian city of Skopje in 1910. At the age of 19, she became a missionary to Calcutta, India. After almost twenty years there, she heard God calling her to the poorest of the poor. She formed "The Missionaries of Charity" in 1950 and committed to serve the poor masses of Calcutta. The primary task of the Missionaries of Charity was to take care of those whom nobody was prepared to look after, such as the homeless and infirmed. Mother Teresa lived a simple life of poverty for many years in Calcutta, saying that when she ministered to the poorest and most hopeless, "Each one of them is Jesus in disguise." She was committed to a life of obedience to Jesus' commands and was a champion of the broken and hurting. On February 3, 1994, she was invited to the National Prayer Breakfast in Washington D.C. In attendance were the President and Vice President of the United States, as well as many other powerful and influential world leaders. But when this little woman, barely visible behind the podium, stood up to speak, a sense of awe filled the room. This frail, aging, tiny nun spoke passionately and without fear in defense of the unborn, a position not held by the American administration at that time. The world was powerfully impacted for God's glory as the words of this obedient woman resounded with the power of God.[15] Because she obeyed God's word in the details of her life, Mother Teresa's words did not "fall to the ground;" they held sway over the mightiest of men.

Pure Living Results in a Powerful Life

Eli's sons were wicked men, sinning greatly before the Lord. Their father, the timid priest, did not have the spiritual strength to restrain them, and they brought disgrace upon Israel. The sentence on Eli's sons and the nation of Israel was carried out as follows:

So the Philistines fought, and the Israelites were defeated and every man fled to his tent. The slaughter was very great; Israel lost thirty thousand foot soldiers. The ark of God was captured, and Eli's two sons, Hophni and Phinehas, died. (1 Samuel 4:10-11)

After receiving this news from a messenger returning from the battle, Eli fell over backward and died, which fulfilled the prophesied judgment on the house of Eli.

In contrast, Samuel possessed exactly what was needed for the Israel of his day: integrity. His inner life was in harmony with his outer life. Unlike his doomed predecessors, there were no inconsistencies. Here is what the Lord said concerning Samuel:

I will raise up for myself a faithful priest, who will do according to what is in my heart and mind. I will firmly establish his house, and he will minister before my anointed one always. (1 Samuel 2:35)

There is a desperate need in the body of Christ today for those who are full of Samuel-like integrity. Gifting and character are two different factors that determine our long-term effectiveness in God's kingdom. But strong gifting without integrity is comparable to constructing a beautiful-looking house with faulty building materials and a cracked foundation. The house may look nice on the outside, but it will eventually fall apart and hurt those it was intended to protect. God requires a solid foundation of His character to build upon in our lives so our gifting will bless others according to His purpose. Although we should certainly attempt to increase our skill level in that which God has given us to do, we should work even more diligently to increase our level of integrity so we can be useful to the very end of our lives.

Because he was pure before God, Samuel was powerful before men. When he walked into the town of Bethlehem to anoint one of Jesse's sons to be the next king of Israel, the elders of the town trembled at his presence (1 Samuel 16:4). Later, toward the end of his life, Samuel asked a question of the Israelites that revealed the outstanding purity that had marked his life. Confronting the nation of Israel he said:

> *Here I stand. Testify against me in the presence of the LORD and his anointed. Whose ox have I taken? Whose donkey have I taken? Whom have I cheated? Whom have I oppressed? From whose hand have I accepted a bribe to make me shut my eyes? If I have done any of these, I will make it right.* (1 Samuel 12:3)

The Israelites unanimously confessed that Samuel had been guiltless before them in his conduct throughout the course of his life.

People, like Samuel, who are full of integrity and have nothing to hide, are confident in executing God's will. Almost twenty years ago, a dear friend of mine, Kurt Mähler, who himself is a man of integrity, spoke a scripture to me that has been a guiding force in my life. He quoted 2 Corinthians 3:4-6:

> *Such confidence as this is ours through Christ before God. Not that we are competent in ourselves to claim anything for ourselves, but our competence comes from God. He has made us competent as ministers of the new covenant—not of the letter but of the Spirit; for the letter kills, but the Spirit gives life.*

The evil one conspires together with our sinful nature to steal our confidence in God. He knows that a confident believer is dangerous to the kingdom of darkness. Many Christians in our day are bound by shame and insecurity in their walk with God because of the secret sins of their hearts. For men in particular, it is often in the arena of sexual misconduct, whether it is Internet pornography, lustful thoughts, or some other deviant behavior. Sin that initially promises to comfort becomes a source of great shame and hinders us from being a driving force for God's glory. Drawing the connection between hidden sin and lack of confidence should inspire us to live before God with sincerity. Then we can walk before men with boldness.

Several years ago, Dr. Charles Davis, a spiritual father of mine, told a group of our leaders about a situation concerning integrity that occurred during the mid-1980s. A crisis that resulted in upheaval and uncertainty developed at the church in Waco, Texas, that I later attended. Sexual impropriety involving the recently fired senior pastor and several church members was painfully revealed to the shocked and reeling congregation. There was an acute need for an interim pastor to help them weather the storm, and the pastoral search committee asked Dr. Davis to consider whether he would be the right man for this assignment. One question they were quite interested in, due to the current crisis, was whether or not he walked in sexual purity. He replied to them with confidence and sincerity, "I would not be embarrassed if my wife saw a video of my thought life." He was offered the position and helped the church navigate the troubled waters of that season. By walking in integrity in the secret places of his heart, Dr. Davis was ready, just as Samuel, to lead God's people out of trouble and into a new season of fruitfulness.

Integrity speaks of the intactness or purity of something. Søren Kierkegaard, a nineteenth century philosopher and theologian, defined it well in the title of his book, *Purity of Heart is to Will One Thing*.[16] Similarly, God found a man in Samuel who willed one thing to the very end of his life - God's glory. Paul the Apostle warned, *"But I am afraid that just as*

Eve was deceived by the serpent's cunning, your minds may somehow be led astray from your sincere and pure devotion to Christ" (2 Corinthians 11:3). Marriage, family and financial concerns progress over the course of life and complicate daily living. It would benefit us greatly to cultivate a continual evaluation of our current season of life. By observing what has changed since the previous season, we can seek to avoid the complexities that cause our hearts to grow cold. Hardness of heart can be deceiving since it is not always a result of blatant sin, but a combination of little compromises. Areas such as neglecting daily time with God, the acquiring of material wealth, and losing contact with life-giving relationships will hinder us from living on the godly "edge" of new personal growth.

If we fail to actively pursue purity of heart, a natural drift can occur that leads us far from a resting place in God. Dwight Edwards, my college pastor while I attended Texas A&M, spoke during my senior year about this spiritual drift that can occur in our lives. He shared that many people, though fervent for God during their college years, were not making any significant spiritual impact soon after graduation. These words struck me like a heavy blow to the chest, and I went to my apartment to seek God. Closing the door to my room, I knelt before God and asked Him what would keep me from being another casualty of a drifting heart. He spoke tenderly and firmly one word - *choices*. From that day on, I have attempted to make choices against the grain of social drift so that I might stay on the "edge" of new growth in my relationship with God. This process is one I am committed to for the rest of my life. Those who continue to be fervent for God and full of spiritual impact must make constant choices of obedience and willingly surrender to new levels of sacrifice. If we have stumbled along the way, God invites us to repent and return to an active pursuit of Him. He is exceedingly gracious to reveal to us where we have drifted and will send His purity on the earnest one like new fallen snow. The reward of a pure heart like

Samuel's is the joy of knowing God "face-to-face" and the honor of leaving a legacy for the next generation of believers to build upon.

CHAPTER 12

FINDING THOSE WITH A SHEPHERD'S HEART

When someone in whom we have invested time, resources, and energy dishonors God by their sinful choices, it can cause waves of pain and discouragement. There is a temptation to pull back from our own intimate pursuit of God and nurse our wounds. Instead of moving forward into the next season of life with hope, this disappointment can result in a paralysis of spirit. Samuel experienced this type of hardship in his relationship with Saul, the first king of Israel. The people of Israel desired to become like the nations around them and demanded Samuel to petition God for a king. Fully aware of the destructive consequences of this decision, God gave them what they wanted in the person of King Saul. He was described as, *"...an impressive young man without equal among the Israelites--a head taller than any of the others"* (1 Samuel 9: 2). Saul, however, was plagued with insecurity that caused him to shrink back in indecision and fear when he should have pressed forward into victory. At other times, this same insecurity caused him to move forward in pride and presumption when he had been commanded to wait for God's timing.

Samuel first met Saul, son of Kish, while Saul was searching for his father's missing donkeys (1 Samuel 9:18). Samuel took him aside and explained that God had chosen him to be king. Tall and handsome, Saul answered Samuel with self deprecation, revealing the deep-seated insecurity that was the source of his controlling and impulsive leadership. Throughout his lengthy rule, he refused to avail himself of the many opportunities to repent and be healed. As a result, Saul was ultimately rejected by God and forfeited the kingship. Samuel, who had invested his heart and soul in Saul, was deeply wounded and lost in disappointment. After a night of grieving prayer, the Lord spoke to Samuel and declared:

> *How long will you mourn for Saul, since I
> have rejected him as king over Israel? Fill
> your horn with oil and be on your way; I am
> sending you to Jesse of Bethlehem. I have
> chosen one of his sons to be king.* (1 Samuel
> 16:1)

Samuel was liberated from his despair and immediately
went to Jesse's house in Bethlehem to anoint the future leader
of Israel.

Saul met all of the external qualifications that people
required in a leader, but his heart was not right before God.
The true prerequisite for leading Israel was being a man after
God's own heart. After this great disappointment, Samuel was
finally led to the true spiritual leader of Israel, David the
shepherd.

As a church planter, this proves to me that our hope for
establishing new churches cannot depend upon a certain gifted
person, but upon God alone. We must look to Him and then
persevere until God's men and women come along. The
church plants that I have participated in have initially drawn a
few people with strong leadership gifting. However, they often did not possess the humility or desire required to become a
true shepherd of God's people. When those with much initial
promise for kingdom advancement did not achieve what
appeared to be their full potential, I, like Samuel, experienced
profound disappointment. Persevering through these disappointments has required me to consistently remind myself of
one important fact. God's work does not depend on the gifting
of any one individual, but on the person of Jesus, the true
cornerstone. Through the faith and perseverance of the church
planter, God will ultimately raise up those who will carry the
work to a new level.

God Doesn't Have Spiritual Grandchildren

Although Samuel appeared to be blameless regarding his own character, there was a troubling development toward the end of his life. We read:

> *When Samuel grew old, he appointed his sons as judges for Israel. The name of his firstborn was Joel and the name of his second was Abijah, and they served at Beersheba. But his sons did not walk in his ways. They turned aside after dishonest gain and accepted bribes and perverted justice.* (1 Samuel 8:1-3)

Samuel lived above reproach, but his sons did not follow his lead. What could have caused this lack of spiritual transfer? It appears that although Samuel's sons knew the acts of God through their father, they did not develop a personal relationship with God by knowing His ways for themselves. They saw what God did through their father's ministry, but they did not come to know their father's intimate friend, the Lord Almighty.

What happened in Samuel's case is not without precedent in the biblical narrative. The Psalmist declared, *"He made known his ways unto Moses, his acts unto the children of Israel"* (Psalm 103:7). Moses knew the *ways* of the Lord, but the desert-bound Israelites knew only God's powerful *acts*. As a result, when testing came and the power of God seemed to withdraw, the Israelites became bitter and turned away from God. The examples of both Samuel and Moses challenge us to pause and consider our own relationship with God. While spending time around God's people, we will see His acts of power and mercy, but we must consistently draw near to God in a private place in order to walk with Him for the long haul. Over the years, I have known people who had powerful experiences with God, yet sometime later they abandoned their relationship with God and His people. A primary reason for this outcome, I believe, was that they failed to develop their own personal relationship with God as a safeguard from bitterness and hardness of heart. As a result, they were unable to process their disappointments properly. When things did not occur the way they desired, they ended up blaming God and others.

Several years ago, a friend of mine was certain that God had revealed that he was to marry a certain person. When it did not happen as he thought, he became bitter and defensive instead of trusting in God's character. Eventually, he walked away from his relationship with God, and I was greatly troubled. As I pondered this in my heart, I began to understand that his hope was not in God; it was in a result that he wanted God to produce for him. When God speaks, we should believe it with all of our hearts and act in faith. However, if it doesn't come to pass the way we had envisioned, we must ultimately submit to God's everlasting wisdom and continue to place our hope in His goodness.

Sooner or later during our spiritual journey, a time of testing from the Lord will come. The question we must face is whether or not we will be prepared for it. Each day is an opportunity to train for the trials of the future. Before and during the trail, the choice of the people whom we chose to associate with is vital, but we are also responsible to cultivate our own connection with God. In order to be securely grounded in our faith, we need both faith-filled community – a circle of friends - and we need solitude with God. Simple daily decisions such as meditating on God's character, refusing to blame others when difficulties come, and staying in relationship with life-giving people will have a wonderful impact on our future. Those who spiritually flourish in the long run are those who choose with the Psalmist to say, *"But as for me, it is good to be near God. I have made the Sovereign LORD my refuge; I will tell of all your deeds"* (Psalm 73: 28).

Samuel chose to be near God in this way, and his life still speaks to us today.

SECTION 7

DAVID - A MAN AFTER GOD'S OWN HEART

All that is not eternal is eternally out of date.
- C.S. Lewis, The Four Loves

King David has captured the hearts and minds of readers for thousands of years. No figure in Old Testament literature has inspired the hearts of people more than this ancient King of Israel. From Michelangelo's statue at the Accademia Gallery in Florence, Italy, to twentieth century movies starring Gregory Peck and Richard Gere, David has been a subject of fascination for many generations. He was a passionate man, a shepherd, a warrior, and a king. David had a lifelong obsession with knowing and loving his God. In his companion to the gospel, Luke states, *"After removing Saul, he [God] made David their king. He testified concerning him: 'I have found David son of Jesse a man after my own heart; he will do everything I want him to do'"* (Acts 13:22). David did not merely know about God, he became deeply familiar with all His ways. This divine love was so powerful that it drove him and colored everything he did. David's relationship with God was so devout that the Lord referred to him time and again as *"David, my servant."* God had found someone He could identify with because David was His beloved friend.

David penned the verse: *"One thing I ask of the LORD, this is what I seek: That I may dwell in the house of the LORD all the days of my life, to gaze upon the beauty of the LORD and to seek him in his temple"* (Psalm 27:4). His treasure was not silver or gold, but the Lord God Almighty. Throughout the course of David's life, his gaze continually returned to the Holy One of Israel.

A couple whom I have known and loved for many years exemplify this lifelong pursuit after God's heart. Darrell and Margie Atwood fell in love and got married when they were teenagers in 1953. They received Christ at a young age and have been serving Him for close to sixty years. The Atwoods have taught for decades about the victorious new life we have in Christ. They have also invested countless hours in seeing this generation of young people established in the Lord and sent to the nations. Whether they share in a small group or teach at a large gathering, they always speak with tears of joy and thankfulness, and at times are nearly unable to finish. These tears at the mention of the name of Jesus are as genuine as a new believer weeping over the forgiveness of his sins for the first time. While praying with Darrell, I have been deeply touched, as he has wept for the children in his city to come to know Jesus. After so many years of seeking God, he and Margie have a heart-knowledge of the love of God and are continually captivated by Him. Like David, Darrell and Margie's hearts are soft towards God and more in love with Him in their final season of life than at the beginning.

After King Saul's failure of leadership, God instructed Samuel to go and anoint a son of Jesse as the next monarch of Israel. Jesse had his sons arranged and ready for inspection soon after Samuel's arrival in Bethlehem. Eliab, the eldest son and pride of his father's heart, stood before the prophet, who was convinced that Eliab was the anointed of God. But the Lord told Samuel:

> *Do not consider his [Eliab's] appearance or his height, for I have rejected him. The LORD does not look at the things man looks at. Man looks at the outward appearance, but the LORD looks at the heart.* (1 Samuel 16:7)

Samuel then observed the remaining sons who stood before him and was perplexed, knowing that none of them was God's man. Oddly enough, the youngest son of Jesse was not in this line-up. David was out in the desert with a flock of sheep. Though seemingly not favored by his father, David was favored by God to lead Israel.

David was a young shepherd alone in the Judean wilderness, tending to his father's sheep. Living in this vast and lonely place, he cultivated a deep relationship with the Lord his God. In the absence of human contact, he became very familiar with the voice of the Almighty and became one of His intimate friends. God's eye was upon David, and God was impressed with this shepherd boy of Israel. Armed with the knowledge of God's father heart, David was enabled to protect his sheep by killing a lion and a bear. The selflessness David displayed while tending his sheep reminded the Lord of His own heart; He had finally found His man. David proved faithful in this small assignment, and God saw that he was prepared for a greater level of leadership (Luke 16:10 and 19:17). David was called in by Samuel and anointed to be the next king of Israel, but there were still many years of preparation ahead.

CHAPTER 13

THE PREPARATORY YEARS

Run to the Battle

After tending the sheep, the next assignment for David came in the form of the Philistine giant, Goliath. This enormous man from Gath had taunted the Army of Israel for many days and spoken against their God. He issued a challenge for one of Israel's number to come out and fight him in hand-to-hand combat. Dismayed and terrified, no one took him up on his offer and Saul, the current King of Israel, was paralyzed with fear. During this time, David was sent by his father on a reconnaissance mission to bring provisions to his brothers. But his brothers despised and scorned David, revealing their deep-seated animosity toward their youngest sibling. However, when he found out about the mocking giant, David's blood began to boil. He was incensed that this "uncircumcised Philistine" would malign the name of his God. David approached King Saul and offered his services, but Saul was initially resistant to his proposal. Finally, the shamed king consented and offered David his fighting equipment. Saul's armor was much too cumbersome, and the son of Jesse exchanged it for five smooth stones. David ran to the battle to meet his massive foe, who was hurling insults at the young shepherd boy. The account continues:

> *As the Philistine moved closer to attack him, David ran quickly toward the battle line to meet him. Reaching into his bag and taking out a stone, he slung it and struck the Philistine on the forehead. The stone sank into his forehead, and he fell facedown on the ground. So David triumphed over the Philistine with a sling and a stone; without a*

> *sword in his hand he struck down the*
> *Philistine and killed him.* (1 Samuel 17:48-50)

David ran headlong into the battle willing to die for the glory of his Heavenly King. He was free of fear and hesitation, which stood in sharp contrast to the other Israelites of his day. He possessed an all-consuming zeal to see justice done as a result of his intimacy with God.

When we enter boldly into God's presence, our actions result in a holy boldness in all that we do for Him. Neglecting the free access we have before God's throne will result in an anemic witness for Him. Regarding the last days of human history, we read, *"...the people who know their God will display strength and take action"* (Daniel 11:32b - NASB). As Goliath taunted the armies of Israel, in our day, Satan taunts the body of Christ and blasphemes the name of our God. The same voice of fear and intimidation that ridiculed the armies of Israel is shouting in our day. Only an extravagant, David-like love for God will enable us to overcome fear and run to the battle to advance God's kingdom in the twenty-first century. We must be a people who are more concerned with His fame and glory than with our own comfort and security. He is calling out those who are deeply affected by the thought of His name being blasphemed, and distraught at the thought of people dying without the knowledge of Him. The generation God is bringing forth will not fear what the world fears, but will fear God alone. Mere *head* knowledge about God will not cause us to storm the gates of the enemy, but *heart* knowledge of God's kindness and generosity will lead us to do great exploits in His name. God's people will willingly volunteer for the glory of His kingdom (Psalm 110:3), and the knowledge of God's glory will cover the earth as the waters cover the seas (Habakkuk 2:14).

Worshipper of God, Deliverer of Men

Mike Bickle, president and director of the International House of Prayer in Kansas City, often shares about his lifelong desire to be a worshiper of God and a deliverer of men. This statement of desire has impacted me so strongly that it has become a prayer of mine through the years. Our oldest son's name, Jude Knight, literally means "Praise Warrior". My wife Sarah and I pray nightly over him that he would be a man who worships God with all his heart and delivers men from the kingdom of darkness. Worship and deliverance are clearly portrayed in David's life through his relationship with his predecessor, King Saul. Saul blatantly disobeyed God and failed to completely destroy the Amalekites, arch-enemies of Israel. As a result, the Spirit of God left Saul and an evil spirit tormented him. Saul became desperate and searched for a way to gain relief from his intense suffering. His attendants advised him to find someone who could play the harp and help bring deliverance from his distress. David's skill in harp playing was mentioned to the king, and as a result, Saul brought him to the palace. We read, *"Whenever the spirit from God came upon Saul, David would take his harp and play. Then relief would come to Saul; he would feel better, and the evil spirit would leave him"* (1 Samuel 16: 23). Saul was delivered from demonic assault through worship and experienced temporary relief. David's praise not only empowered him to fight the Lord's battles, but also enabled him to lead many people to freedom in God.

The life and songs of the late Keith Green, a twentieth-century David, have strongly influenced me throughout the course of my life and have helped me to develop a worshipful and obedient heart. While growing up in the 1970s, my mother played his records, and it was through listening to albums such as, *No Compromise* and *Songs for the Shepherd* that I began to understand what being a true worshiper of God really meant. While singing along with Keith, I felt as if I was listening to

David himself worshipping in the desert while tending the sheep. Not only did Keith Green sing beautiful songs to God, but he also obeyed God with all of his heart. He and his wife, Melody fed and housed the poor, stood against injustice, and called people to obedience in every area of their lives. One particular song of Keith's that has continually challenged me to be a true worshipper of God is entitled *To Obey is Better Than Sacrifice*. May God stir your heart as you read these words:

> *To obey is better than sacrifice,*
> *I don't need your money, I want your life.*
> *And I hear you say that I'm coming back soon,*
> *But you act like I'll never return.*
> *Well you speak of grace and my love so sweet,*
> *How you thrive on milk, but reject my meat,*
> *And I can't help weeping of how it will be,*
> *If you keep on ignoring my words.*
> *Well you pray to prosper and succeed,*
> *But your flesh is something I just can't feed.*
> *To obey is better than sacrifice.*
> *I want more than Sunday and Wednesday nights,*
> *'Cause if you can't come to me every day,*
> *Then don't bother coming at all.*[17]

The last stanza was controversial, however, this song succinctly conveys the all-consuming pursuit of God for which Keith always strove. By the time Keith died in a plane crash in 1982 at the age of 28, this obedient man had discipled a generation of believers to be worshippers of God and deliverers of men.

A Lesson in Spiritual Authority

David had tremendous success in all that Saul gave him to do, ironically causing Saul to turn against him. David had already been anointed by Samuel to be king, but Saul was still "the Lord's anointed," as David called him, because he remained on the throne. The biblical narrator writes:

> *Whatever Saul sent him to do, David did it so successfully that Saul gave him a high rank in the army. This pleased all the people, and Saul's officers as well. When the men were returning home after David had killed the Philistine, the women came out from all the towns of Israel to meet King Saul with singing and dancing, with joyful songs and with tambourines and lutes. As they danced, they sang:*
>
> > *"Saul has slain his thousands, and David his tens of thousands."*
>
> *Saul was very angry; this refrain galled him. "They have credited David with tens of thousands," he thought, "but me with only thousands. What more can he get but the kingdom?" And from that time on Saul kept a jealous eye on David.* (1 Samuel 18:5-9)

King Saul was against David and sought to kill him in order to eliminate the threat to his kingdom.

We can learn a great deal by observing the godly trust David exhibited during these difficult years. The future king's understanding of spiritual authority is a model we would do well to imitate. One day while David was playing the harp, Saul hurled a spear at him in an attempt to pin him to the wall (1 Samuel 18:11). Saul was physically without equal in Israel. His violent act must have been a terrifying experience for David, filling him with a tremendous sense of rejection and fear. David was later forced to flee from Saul, who chased David through the desert like hunted prey. The long-standing wound of rejection from his father Jesse was exposed as this father figure, Saul, sought to eliminate him. Lesser men would have allowed bitterness and rage to fill their hearts, but David continued to rely on God as his defender. He was sorely tested but refused to take matters into his own hands. He was proven faithful and pleased his Heavenly Father's heart.

Saul finally caught up with David in the desert of En Gedi where we pick up the account:

> *So, Saul took three thousand chosen men from all Israel and set out to look for David and his men near the Crags of the Wild Goats. He came to the sheep pens along the way; a cave was there, and Saul went in to relieve himself. David and his men were far back in the cave. The men said, "This is the day the LORD spoke of when he said to you, 'I will give your enemy into your hands for you to deal with as you wish.'" Then David crept up unnoticed and cut off a corner of Saul's robe. Afterward David was conscience-stricken for having cut off a corner of his robe. He said to his men, "The LORD forbid that I should do such a thing to my master, the Lord's anointed, or lift my hand against him; for he is the anointed of the LORD." (1 Samuel 24:2-7)*

David had already been anointed by Samuel to be the next king of Israel. Moreover, Saul had continually betrayed David's trust after promising that he would not harm him. In addition, the fight was unreasonably lopsided, as Saul led three thousand fighting men against David's small band. Saul, however, had walked into a trap, and David's men were challenging him to take revenge against this tyrant. David, however, exhibited extraordinary self-restraint and displayed a remarkable amount of godly character. Though the temptation for reprisal was strong, David understood and continually re-affirmed the principle that protection and promotion are from the Lord.

David was so spiritually sensitive that he was "conscience-stricken" for merely cutting off a piece of Saul's robe. This future ruler knew that unless he respected the authority that God had given Saul in his life, he would never carry authority with the power that God intended for him. Had David taken things into his own hands, as his predecessor Saul had, his name would not have endured throughout the generations. To possess true spiritual authority, we should be self-controlled and wait for God's timing. We would be wise to resist human reasoning, as David did, regarding our reputation and advancement in the kingdom of God. The days of preparation were finally drawing to a close and God was ready to establish David's kingdom.

CHAPTER 14

KING OF ISRAEL

David displayed numerous godly attributes during his reign that distinguished him from so many of his contemporaries. He had learned absolute, unqualified dependence on God in the desert, and as a result, he practiced that same dependence in the palace. Moses spent four decades in the desert being prepared to lead God's people. King David was also prepared for rulership while surviving in the desert. Like Moses before him, David encountered God's presence and provision while tending sheep. After years in the crucible of the wilderness, the time had finally come for God to exalt his man. The Israelites had been slaughtered on Mount Gilboa by the Philistines, and an Amalekite ran to David to inform him of the death of King Saul and his son Jonathan, who had been a close friend of David. He took up a lament and said:

> *Your glory O Israel, lies slain on the heights.*
> *How the mighty have fallen! Saul and*
> *Jonathan – in life they were loved and*
> *gracious, and in death they were not parted.*
> *They were swifter than eagles, they were*
> *stronger than lions.* (2 Samuel 1:19, 23)

David had taught his men how to worship and now he showed them how to mourn. David knew the proper time to laugh and to grieve. He had a wonderful sense of timing and understood the concept of honor well.

Honor is undervalued in our day, and we must recapture this virtue in order to fully experience God's divine presence. David refused to succumb to the temptation of rejoicing over Saul's death; instead he genuinely grieved over the loss of the Lord's anointed. He was more concerned with God and His kingdom than with his own personal feelings. David was after God's own heart, and God saw to it that His servant had success in whatever endeavor he undertook. After Saul and Jonathan's death, David again exhibited self-control when Ish-Bosheth, son of Saul, attempted to assert his claim on the kingship (2 Samuel 2:8-4:5). David waited patiently and was finally anointed by the people as king over Judah. He reigned in Hebron for six years before the remaining tribes of Israel acknowledged David as their king. David conquered Jerusalem and ruled the next thirty-three years over the entire nation of Israel from the city that bears his name, the "City of David."

David did not assume that he automatically understood how to fight each battle. He continually sought God's wisdom and demonstrated humility by inquiring of the Lord before he waged war. David's humility allowed him to expand his influence as he met with great success on the battlefield. We read, *"So David did as the Lord commanded him, and he struck down the Philistines, all the way from Gibeon to Gezer"* (2 Samuel 5:25).

We try to emulate this attribute of dependence that David modeled in our own church leadership meetings. We do not make major decisions before praying and waiting on the Lord. When we hear what He is saying about a particular decision, it is possible to move forward with confidence. If the decision is crucial, we often accompany prayer with fasting. Fasting does not change God; it changes us and prepares us to hear what He is saying. Through abstaining from food, we are drawn to Him and freed from sin's deceitful influence. We do not want our own plan, but we are seeking God and listening for His voice. There is no maturity level where we know God's will without seeking Him, because the will of God flows out of the daily knowledge of Him. Only He knows the hearts of men, as well as the proper time and the right way to implement each decision. We have saved ourselves many pains through seeking divine wisdom before we act. The old hymn says it best:

What a Friend we have in Jesus,
All our sins and griefs to bear!
What a privilege to carry
Everything to God in prayer!
O what peace we often forfeit,
O what needless pain we bear
All because we do not carry
Everything to God in prayer.[18]

Providing that we are in it for His pleasure, we will have success God's way, and that is all that really matters.

Another attribute of God exhibited by David was his delight in showing kindness. After his ascension to the throne, we read, *"David asked, 'Is there anyone still left of the house of Saul to whom I can show kindness for Jonathan's sake?"* (2 Samuel 9:1). David was rich in spirit with the kindness and generosity of God, and he needed an outlet for his full heart. Following his inquiry, David found out about a grandson of Jonathan's named Mephibosheth. This man was crippled from an accident that occurred when the tragic news about Saul and Jonathan's death came from the battlefield. David instructed Saul's servant Ziba to bring Mephibosheth to him at the palace:

> *"Don't be afraid," David said to him, "for I will surely show kindness to you for the sake of your father Jonathan. I will restore to you all the land that belonged to Saul and you will always eat at my table"* (2 Samuel 9:7)

God's benevolent goodness set David free from a scarcity mentality and created in him a generosity of spirit. David, reflecting God's overwhelming abundance, delighted to be kind and to care for the poor.

A faithful friend to our movement of churches is Karen (Alford) Mähler, who, like King David, has continually demonstrated godly concern for the poor and the orphan. We met after I moved to Waco, Texas, in December 1989 to attend the Master's Commission training school at Highland Baptist Church led by Jimmy Seibert. Karen was one of my fellow students in this school, which was created to develop sincere disciples of Jesus. She has always been an extremely gentle and low-key woman, but I was impressed from the start with the intensity of love and concern that Karen possessed for the poor. As far as she was concerned, a person's worldly pedigree was irrelevant. If they needed love and care, she was available to be the hands and feet of Jesus. During worship and prayer in our training school, she would often kneel, pleading for the ones who did not know of the Savior's love. She made me uncomfortable because I was jealous of her tender heart. I had yet to learn the key to loving that she knew so well. She understood the spiritual secret of tapping into the heart of Jesus, for His heart is full of compassion and mercy. Our love is superficial, and He must show us our spiritual bankruptcy so that we will be conduits of His limitless supply.

Karen finished the training school and continued loving the people around her while waiting to be released to the nations. She served children in a poorer community of Waco until a church planting team could be raised up to go to the nations. She did not wait to become an overseas missionary before extravagantly loving these children and their families. After a year and a half she traveled with Antioch's first church planting team to Siberia. Soon after returning from a ten-month stint in the city of Ulan Ude, she married Kurt Mähler. They then went to the Muslim world and spent years in Afghanistan and the Middle East caring for the poor and unreached with the undying love of their Redeemer. Kurt and Karen are examples to us all that to love Jesus fully is to love people with all of our hearts.

The Righteous Fall...But Rise Again

King David experienced great success as he led the army of Israel and defeated all of his enemies. At the very height of his power, with the kingdom firmly established, David let down his guard. The celebrated leader of Israel, held in awe by the people he ruled, lost his edge. The telling account reads:

> *In the spring, when the kings go off to war, David sent Joab out with the king's men and the whole Israelite army. They destroyed the Ammonites and besieged Rabbah. <u>But David remained in Jerusalem</u>* (2 Samuel 11:1, *emphasis mine*)

In the midst of triumph, David became calloused, and he was swept away by a drifting heart. He was in the wrong place at the wrong time and was seduced by the sin of adultery. David got up in the middle of the night, walked to the edge of his rooftop and saw Bathsheba, wife of Uriah the Hittite, bathing. David was driven by sinful desire, and he used his power in an ungodly manner to get what he wanted. When David discovered that Bathsheba was pregnant, he tried to cover his sin instead of confessing it, and he ended up murdering a loyal subject, Uriah.

This adulterous affair with Bathsheba reveals the depravity of David's heart apart from God. Uriah the Hittite is mentioned as one of David's mighty men (1 Chronicles 11:41). This was a select group of warriors with whom David had been to battle numerous times. Uriah had clearly distinguished himself on the battlefield. He was no stranger to King David, but was a close and trusted friend who had committed his life to protecting his king. David and Uriah had most likely shared stories of victory together around the campfire while living as a band of brothers on the battlefield. However, David's lust drove him to kill his faithful friend. Not only was Uriah a valiant warrior; he was a loyal man. When David tried to deceive him by sending him home to sleep with Bathsheba, Uriah refused, sleeping on a mat outside his house with the servants. Uriah explained:

> *The ark and Israel and Judah are staying in tents, and my master Joab and my lord's men are camped in the open fields. How could I go to my house to eat and drink and lie with my wife? As surely as you live, I will not do such a thing!* (2 Samuel 11:11)

These words alone should have shamed David and awakened him to his depraved state, but in his backslidden condition, he did not relent. Uriah was a righteous man, committed in his heart to God's army and his commander Joab, but David sent Uriah back to the battle lines carrying his own death sentence in a sealed letter from David to Joab. Shakespeare could not have written a greater tragedy.

God eventually sent the prophet Nathan to rebuke David, and the king finally repented. Only David's deep revelation of the mercy and grace of God kept him from being crushed with guilt. David placed his confidence in the great God of men, whose mercy is new every morning for those who look to Him. We catch a glimpse of the totality of God's forgiveness after the death of David and Bathsheba's firstborn. The account continues, *"Then David comforted his wife Bathsheba, and he went to her and lay with her. She gave birth to a son, and they named him Solomon. The LORD loved him"* (2 Samuel 12:24). This is a poignant illustration of God's forgiving nature. There was no remembrance of David's sin, or even a hint of God holding a grudge. God had richly forgiven him, delighted in being merciful, and stated His unconditional love for Solomon.

In our feelings of condemnation about our sin, we often make God in our own image and likeness instead of worshipping Him for who He is. We imagine Him as petty and vindictive, but He is not tainted as we are by the sinful nature. He is the most secure, loving being in the universe, and He delights in giving mercy. We should stand in awe and worship Him realizing that He is ready to forgive and move forward when we quit hiding and choose to repent. In His faithful way, He will restore our lost years and give us an abundant harvest in spite of our failures (Joel 2:25).

Leaving a Spiritual Legacy

Our lives affect the generations that follow, and for those who pursue righteousness, there is a sure reward. David lived wholeheartedly for God, which resulted in a vast spiritual legacy. David's life proves that those who live wholeheartedly for God will affect the generations to come. May we live as a springboard to those who come after us and make the way less traveled easier for them to find. Paul gave this testimony, *"For when David had served God's purpose in his own generation, he fell asleep [died]"* (Acts 13:36). David was a man with a burning heart for God who won mighty victories and endured great moral defeat. He was God's man to the very end, and as a result, he has been rewarded with a legacy that includes Jesus, the King of Kings.

SECTION 8

JONATHAN - EVERY DAVID NEEDS ONE

It is better to have a hundred friends than a hundred rubles.
– Russian Proverb

The chronicle of King David's life is a true joy to read, and one cannot help being impressed with his heart for God. While studying the account of David, we also come to appreciate Jonathan's love for God and commitment to David. As the son of King Saul, Jonathan was the natural heir to the throne of Israel. However, his father had forfeited his right to the kingship, and David had been anointed king of Israel in his place. Saul was aware of this and sought to kill David, first in the palace and then in the desert. In stark contrast to his father, Jonathan committed to loving and protecting David, even against his father's wishes. He spoke well of David to his father Saul and said:

> *Let not the king do wrong to his servant*
> *David; he has not wronged you, and what he*
> *has done has benefitted you greatly. He took*
> *his life in his hands when he killed the*
> *Philistine. The LORD won a great victory for*
> *all Israel, and you saw it and were glad. Why*
> *then would you do wrong to an innocent man*
> *like David by killing him for no reason?* (1
> Samuel 19:4-5)

It required an astounding degree of humility for Jonathan to defend the one who would ascend to the throne in his place. But he was a covenant-maker and a covenant-keeper, just like his God.

CHAPTER 15

COVENANT RELATIONSHIP

Sean Richmond is the man whom I have had the honor of walking with most consistently in ministry through the years. We first met in the summer of 1989 when he was a college senior and I was a recent college graduate. Since I have known him, Sean has always possessed a deep passion for God and a hunger for the Holy Spirit. There soon developed between us a close friendship in which we spurred one another on to wholeheartedness in godly pursuits. We have also shared numerous powerful encounters with the Lord in worship, prayer and witness.

Sean and I have had numerous experiences sharing Christ, going to the nations together, and taking risks in God. We have laughed together, cried together and have walked side by side for over twenty years. We are currently laboring together as lead pastors of sister congregations in Massachusetts. It has been a true privilege to walk in long-standing partnership with him, and I owe an immense debt of gratitude to Sean and his wife Laura, who are both faithful friends. They have encouraged and believed in me when I have been in desperate places, and I have had the joy of returning the favor in their time of need.

Sean and I traveled to New Mexico for a vacation and a visit to his sister's family during the summer of 1991. We were full of zeal for Jesus and spent hours in prayer and worship as we drove to our destination. After arriving, we played golf, went to a football game, and relaxed in the beautiful mountains that surrounded his sister's home. We also set aside a day for a personal retreat and spent the entire morning separately worshiping, praying and listening to God's voice in the midst of His creation. We came back together in the afternoon to pray and share what God had spoken to our hearts. It was encouraging to discover that God had spoken to both of us about the relationship between King David and his friend

Jonathan, a bond so strong they sealed it with a covenant. There was a great sense of expectancy that day as we talked and dreamed of how true covenant relationship could be walked out. Neither of us had any idea how closely we would be called to walk in ministry during the years that followed, but God had given us a blueprint to use that has guided our relationship to this day.

Contemporary Western society does not tend to value relationships in the same way as many Eastern cultures. This contrast became evident to me while visiting friends who live in the Middle East. While walking on top of their flat-walled roof one day, I noticed that many of the surrounding homes had rebar projecting upward from the rooftops. My friend Khris explained that rebar was left on top of these buildings to allow for adding an additional floor. The new top-floor apartment was built for the owner's son or daughter after he or she married. This is a prime example of the difference in an Eastern and Western worldview regarding relationships. In America, we value independence so much that it borders on strange if one lives with his or her parents too long after graduation. People with an Eastern mindset, however, place a high value on the family unit, not considering it odd for adult children to live with their parents after marriage. In contrast, there is not a high value of commitment to a locality or relationships in the Western world. Therefore, it would be beneficial to observe God's design for healthy relationships by studying the lives of Jonathan and David.

Some modern scholars have falsely asserted that these two royal friends had a homosexual relationship. This can be partly attributed to the lack of understanding in contemporary society of how relationships functioned in David and Jonathan's cultural context. For example, even today, men are much more affectionate with each other in many Eastern cultures than men in Western society. Jonathan and David were knit together in heart and fully committed to each other's success, no matter how high the cost to themselves. Their relationship illustrated the Lord Jesus' statement recalled by the Apostle John; *"Greater love has no one than this, that he lay down his life for his friends"* (John 15:13). The advancement of God's kingdom is tragically hindered due to a lack of healthy covenant relationships between members of the Body of Christ. As the prolific Christian writer John Stott forcefully stated, "Personal ambition and empire building are hindering the spread of the gospel."[20] When people lay down their own ambitions for the cause of Christ, there is no limit to what God can do through them. God will give an ample supply of His Spirit to those who pray and work together for His glory on earth.

Jonathan and David possessed "relational capital." They had the advantage of a long-term relationship that resulted in the expansion of God's kingdom. Capital is defined as "any form of wealth capable of being employed in the production of more wealth."[21] When godly people develop trust through years of relationship, they enjoy relational capital that enables them to advance God's kingdom with speed and power. Those with a lone ranger mentality do not experience this blessing, a gift that the Psalmist rejoices about:

> *How good and pleasant it is when brothers live together in unity. It is like precious oil poured on the head, running down on Aaron's beard, down upon the collar of his robes. It is as if the dew of Hermon were falling on Mount Zion. For there the LORD bestows his blessing, even life forevermore.* (Psalm 133:1-3)

Most believers desire to know what God is calling them to accomplish through their lives. Although this is important to discern, I would suggest that a more vital question for us to ask is with whom God has called us to partner. God anoints groups of people to accomplish greater purposes than the sum of their parts. It is an honor to have found my tribe, so to speak - a band of brothers who I plan to walk with for the rest of my life. Though we are a flawed and weak people, we have been given to each other to accomplish impossible things for the glory of God. Our hearts are captured with the joyful antici-pation of standing before Jesus with our shared inheritance, the souls of men. We will lay our crowns at His feet as we cele-brate His victory through our frail, but yielded lives. This type of relational capital allowed Jonathan and David to obey God's will and accomplish greater exploits than if they had served in isolation.

Covenant relationships give greater power to every aspect of our lives, as observed in the biblical portrayal of Jonathan even while he was not with David. Let us observe this inspiring account:

> One day Jonathan son of Saul said to the young man bearing his armor, "Come, let's go over to the Philistine outpost on the other side." But he did not tell his father. Jonathan said to his young armor-bearer, "Come, let's go over to the outpost of those uncircumcised fellows. Perhaps the LORD will act in our behalf. Nothing can hinder the LORD from saving, whether by many or by few..." So both of them showed themselves to the Philistine outpost. "Look!" said the Philistines. "The Hebrews are crawling out of the holes they were hiding in." The men of the outpost shouted to Jonathan and his armor-bearer, "Come up to us and we'll teach you a lesson." So Jonathan said to his armor-bearer, "Climb up after me; the LORD has given them into the hand of Israel." Jonathan climbed up, using his hands and feet, with his armor-bearer right behind him. The Philistines fell before

Jonathan, and his armor-bearer followed and killed behind him. In that first attack Jonathan and his armor-bearer killed some twenty men in an area of about half an acre... Then panic struck the whole army - those in the camp and field, and those in the outposts and raiding parties - and the ground shook. It was a panic sent by God. (1 Samuel 14:1-15)

Jonathan possessed a divine love that motivated him to take action on behalf of God. He proved that the Lord had power to deliver a victory "by few" and he had a different spirit than his father Saul. Jonathan was a man of faith, like David, who trusted in God's divine providence and accomplished God's will in spite of the circumstances into which he was born.

CHAPTER 16

MARVELOUS COMRADES

Antioch Ministries International (AMI), the organization that my wife and I are associated with, began in 1988. One of the key prayers of AMI's president Jimmy Seibert and his wife Laura over the years has been, "Lord, give us marvelous comrades who fear your name." Jonathan and David were marvelous comrades who played a significant role in each other's destiny. Each supplied what the other lacked and they enabled one another to overcome adversity and live intentionally. An important provision they supplied each other was friendship. The biblical narrative describes: *"After David had finished talking with Saul, Jonathan became one in spirit with David and he loved him as himself...and Jonathan made a covenant with David because he loved him as himself. Jonathan then took off the robe he was wearing and gave it to David along with his tunic and even his sword, his bow and his belt"* (1 Samuel 18:1-4).

There are precious few who come our way in life with whom we are completely comfortable. In *Anne of Green Gables*, Anne Shirley asserts, "Everyone needs a kindred spirit." God has blessed me with a few of these along the way, but Jesus did not guarantee that we would have our best friends around all of the time. In fact, we must relinquish our right to these friendships when God calls us to obey Him in the advancement of His kingdom on earth. On the other hand, when we seek God and dive into relationships with like-hearted people, we are more apt to encounter true kindred friendships. Enjoying these times of rich companionship is a vital necessity. When we enter a season of relational scarcity, though, we should continue to trust God, knowing that He will provide what we need in due time.

The friendship between Jonathan and David also provided protection from the enemy. David's great success caused Saul to keep a jealous eye on him and to eventually attempt to kill him. The following instance illustrates the importance of committed relationships during dangerous times:

> *Saul told his son Jonathan and all the attendants to kill David. But Jonathan was very fond of David and warned him, "My father Saul is looking for a chance to kill you. Be on your guard tomorrow morning; go into hiding and stay there. I will go out and stand with my father in the field where you are. I'll speak to him about you and will tell you what I find out." Jonathan spoke well of David to Saul his father and said to him, "Let not the king do wrong to his servant David; he has not wronged you, and what he has done has benefitted you greatly." Saul listened to Jonathan and took this oath, "As surely as the LORD lives, David will not be put to death."*
> (1 Samuel 19:1-4; 6)

Jonathan pledged to protect David, even when it put him in possible danger. In the same way, we have an inherent need in our lives for people to protect us through prayer and honest speech while defending us before our adversaries.

Due to our close friendship and shared ministry, a verbal attack on Sean Richmond feels as though it were an attack on me. Defending my brother and clarifying his motives to others is most natural to me because I know that he desires to walk in godly obedience. Sean and I maintain an open dialogue of encouragement as well as rebuke, but we are uncompromising in defense of each other's character. We should never cease to provide this loving service for each other. As we go into battle for the King of Kings, it is not only loving, but also strategic. Satan, the enemy of our souls, desires to destroy our godly friends; but through prayer, love and honest speech, we provide a hedge around them that he cannot overcome.

We must recapture the lost art of protecting each other's reputations in the Body of Christ. There are too many kingdom warriors who have been casualties of "friendly fire." Friendly fire occurs when someone is injured or killed by another person who is fighting for the same country or cause. It is an unintentional tragedy for the soldiers as well as their families. Likewise, my spirit grieves when someone in the Body of Christ sees it as his "ministry" to expose everyone else's faults. In the parable of the weeds and wheat in Matthew 24, Jesus tells of a landowner who warned his servants that they should not try to uproot the weeds interspersed among the heads of grain, or the servants might find themselves uprooting valuable wheat. But, unfortunately, many people in the Body of Christ have been casualties of overzealous weed pullers. This does not pertain to cardinal doctrines that must be defended by the Body of Christ, such as the deity of Christ and salvation by grace through faith, but to those who attack other ministries because of a desire for so called "doctrinal purity" when the issue is actually personal rivalry or conflict. We absolutely need correct theology in the Body of Christ, but doctrine can be truly pure only when we couple the truth that we know with loving deeds of obedience.

Jonathan and David's covenant relationship also provided practical assistance for each other. In the following account we read, *"Jonathan said to David, 'Whatever you want me to do, I'll do for you'"* (1 Samuel 20:4). A vital spiritual service we should perform for our friends is to offer practical assistance with the necessities of life.

In 1998, I initially moved to Boston as part of a team to plant Community of Faith Christian Fellowship, where I currently pastor. We had a running joke that one of the unwritten qualifications for being a church planter should include prior experience as a professional home mover. Moving people into their apartments and houses proved to be one of the most common bonding experiences for our young church. It may have seemed like a trivial matter, but it is difficult to estimate the amount of godly community that was borne through this simple service. An American ideal is to work hard and make enough money to avoid having to ask for help, but this can cause relational poverty. When we overemphasize money and possessions, there is a tendency for us to move toward isolation as we lose our desire and need for community. Through offering ourselves to God and His people first, though, we may not have enough money to hire movers, but we gain the value of relationship through serving each other in practical ways.

The final benefit we observe in Jonathan's relationship with David is encouragement. We read:

> *While David was at Horesh in the Desert of Ziph, he learned that Saul had come out to take his life. And Saul's son Jonathan went to David at Horesh and helped him find strength in God. "Don't be afraid," he said, "My father Saul will not lay a hand on you. You will be king over Israel and I will be second to you. Even my father Saul knows this." The two of them made a covenant before the LORD. Then Jonathan went home, but David remained at Horesh."* (1 Samuel 23:15-18)

As one reads the account of David living among ruthless enemies, his ability to "find strength in the Lord his God" (1 Samuel 30:6) becomes evident. However, there is also an inherent need for believers to receive encouragement from others. A common misperception in spiritual circles is that a mature believer has learned to get all of his needs met in Jesus. While God must be our preeminent source of emotional provision, He has created us with an innate need to receive encouragement and strength from others. This reinforces humility in both the giver and receiver. The one giving the encouragement must look to the interests of another - putting the needs of another above his own - and the receiver must humble himself by admitting his own need.

The instances above illustrate what Jonathan and David provided for each other throughout their covenant relationship, and we should try to follow their example. God desires to ignite movements of people that spread rapidly across the globe through an extravagant commitment to Jesus Christ. The success of these movements is dependent upon covenant relationships between people who are committed to Jesus and the expansion of His kingdom. We must be willing to link our lives together with other imperfect people to attempt impossible things for God's glory. Those who examine their hearts and deal aggressively with prideful and independent attitudes will obtain the blessing of a shared inheritance. Pride and selfish ambition are insidious creatures that must be destroyed in order for us to be joyfully knit with others who are given to godly pursuits.

Spiritually independent people will not be effective in the long term because they are operating without the principle of humility. Several years ago, while asking the Lord to explain the reason for some of my personal trials, He spoke a word to my heart that both humbled me and gave me an eternal perspective. With loving firmness He said, "I am driving pride out of your life, so that I don't have to resist you anymore." It became clear that God would have to resist my relationships and spiritual progress if I lacked humility. God only gives grace to the humble - it is a spiritual law. These trials provided the humility that I needed in order to partner with others in accomplishing great feats in God's name. Let us thank God for the wonderful plans that He has in store for us and ask Him for marvelous comrades, like Jonathan and David, to help us fulfill them.

SECTION 9

ELIJAH - PROPHETIC VOICE

*I'm against sin. I'll kick it as long as I've
got a foot, and I'll fight it as long as I've got a fist.
I'll butt it as long as I've got a head. I'll bite it as
long as I've got a tooth. And when I'm old and
fistless and footless and toothless, I'll gum it till
I go home to Glory and it goes home to perdition!
- William Ashley ("Billy") Sunday, Early 20th
Century American Evangelist*

When we seek to follow God wholeheartedly, what we do will often bring us into conflict with the ways of man. The first account of Elijah reads, *"Now Elijah the Tishbite from Tishbe in Gilead, said to Ahab, 'As the Lord God of Israel lives, whom I serve, there will be neither dew nor rain in the next few years except at my word"* (1 Kings 17:1). God sent the prophet Elijah to confront wicked King Ahab concerning his sinful ways. Elijah pronounced God's judgment in the form of drought and famine, and his proclamation brought Elijah into a spiritual clash with a king of the most unsavory character. God gave Israel numerous opportunities to turn from their depravity, but they persisted in their rebellion. God longed to be merciful, but Israel was unwilling to repent and receive His kindness. The judgment of drought and famine was God's way of calling out to Israel in order to awaken Ahab and his people from their spiritual slumber.

Following these three years of famine, the Lord commanded Elijah to appear before Ahab and promise rain from heaven's storehouses. While en route to the king, he met Obadiah, who was under Ahab's command and whose job it was to scavenge food for Israel's starving livestock. Obadiah was a noble person who had protected one hundred prophets of the Lord during the murderous rampage of Jezebel, the king's wife. The story reads:

So Obadiah went to meet Ahab and told him, and Ahab went to meet Elijah. When he saw Elijah he said to him [Ahab], "Is that you, you troubler of Israel?" "I have not made trouble for Israel," Elijah replied. "But you and your father's family have. You have abandoned the Lord's commands and have followed the Baals..." (1 Kings 18:16-18)

The king rushed to accuse Elijah of being a troublemaker, even though the prophet's conduct and predictions had been righteous. Ahab was a spiritually blind man. He made no correlation between his own sin and the judgment upon Israel. He had completely abandoned the Lord and turned to idolatry, yet he blamed righteous Elijah for Israel's plight. The prophet endured false accusation, but he stood the test of uncompromising faith and paved the way for God's righteousness.

CHAPTER 17

GODLY DEPENDENCE RELEASES SPIRITUAL POWER

Fed by Ravens

Immediately following Elijah's proclamation to Ahab of the impending nationwide drought, we read, *"Then the word of the LORD came to Elijah: Leave here, turn eastward and hide in the Kerith Ravine, east of the Jordan. You will drink from the brook and I have ordered the ravens to feed you there"* (1 Kings 17:2-4). Those who live wholeheartedly for God must be comfortable with receiving their provision from His hand. Our approach to money and possessions is an accurate indicator of the state of our relationship with God. If He is truly our provider, then we will obey for the sake of His name without fear for our material provision.

Jimmy Seibert asked me to join him on the Master's Commission staff beginning in September 1990. The example for financial support we followed during that time in our ministry was that of the nineteenth-century missionary George Mueller. He founded and funded a number of orphanages in England through simple prayer and faith.[22] George did not let anyone except God know of his needs, and he saw miraculous provision throughout his lifetime. This was documented in his autobiography, which was required reading in our training school curriculum.

After agreeing to partner with Jimmy in this ministry, I began to fear for my financial provision. Jimmy and I talked through my concerns, and his words of comfort helped to set me free. Jimmy said, "Jeff, if Laura and I have a loaf of bread, you can have half of it." Knowing that I was not alone in this endeavor, I took the financial risk and have never looked back. God has abundantly provided for me over the years as I have travelled throughout the world to preach the gospel. My wife, Sarah, and I have never lacked for anything we have truly needed, and we have been pleasantly surprised while seeking God's kingdom purposes. We do not check our pocketbook before we step out in faith to obey God. That which He calls us to is often beyond our own abilities and past the limits of our finite understanding. As we obey God, He will never fail to prove Himself as our faithful provider.

Miracle Man

A distinguishing characteristic of Elijah's life and ministry was supernatural power. God does not display His divine power simply to impress people, but to reveal His mercy and open the door of salvation to the lost. We see this illustrated when Elijah became friends with a woman in the village of Zarephath whom God had saved during the famine. Through a miracle decreed by the prophet, God provided for her through an abundant, supernatural supply of flour and oil. Over the course of time, a dilemma arose which posed a great challenge for Elijah. The account reads:

> Some time later the son of the woman who owned the house became ill. He grew worse and worse, and finally stopped breathing. She said to Elijah, "What do you have against me, man of God? Did you come to remind me of my sin and kill my son?" "Give me your son," Elijah replied. He took him from her arms, carried him to the upper room where he was staying, and laid him on his bed. Then he cried out to the LORD, "O LORD my God, have you brought tragedy also upon this widow I am staying with, by causing her son to die?" Then he stretched himself out on the boy three times and cried to the Lord, "O LORD my God, let this boy's life return to him!" The LORD heard Elijah's cry, and the

boy's life returned to him, and he lived. Elijah picked up the child and carried him down from the room into the house. He gave him to his mother and said, "Look, your son is alive!" Then the woman said to Elijah, "Now I know that you are a man of God and that the word of the LORD from your mouth is the truth." (1 Kings 17:17-24)

Having already experienced God's provision, it was only after her son was raised from the dead that this widow fully believed Elijah was God's man. God performs miracles in order to confirm the truth of His message and His messenger. Our conversations with unbelievers need to be confirmed by God's power so they will know that we are from God and that the words from our mouths are the truth.

During the summer of 1991, I was introduced to a revival atmosphere full of God's miracle working power. It was a time of spiritual harvest for many of the liberated nations of Eastern Europe, and the faith level of the people living in this region of the world was extremely high. While ministering in Veliko Turnovo, Bulgaria, God worked so powerfully among us that people would crowd the streets for hours listening to the message of salvation. The healing power of Jesus was on display and was so thick that we needed to pick up our interpreter several times after she fell down in God's presence. One day, after we shared a message on the father heart of God at a local auditorium, we called for those who needed healing to come forward. A young lady approached me wearing glasses and asked me to pray for her eyes. After prayer, I attempted to give her glasses back to her and she gave me an odd look and walked off without them. All that was required for her healing was a mustard seed of faith. During that season, we saw God use His power through the miraculous to save the lost. Each time we preached, God testified to His word by performing miraculous signs, and He drew lost people to Himself in droves. By the end of the week there was not enough room to meet inside in our host's church building, so the celebration moved onto the street. We had fresh appreciation of the scripture that states, *"The disciples were filled with joy and with the Holy Spirit"* (Acts 13:52). This adventure in Eastern Europe illustrated that when people are desperate for Him, God is powerfully drawn to them and He will display His goodness for all to see.

The God Who Answers By Fire

Jezebel led her husband Ahab into idol worship, and she appointed four hundred and fifty prophets of Baal and four hundred prophets of Asherah to serve at the temples designed for Baal. Worship of these foreign gods was a clear violation of the second commandment - "you shall have no other gods before me" - and an affront to God. The prophet Elijah was called on once again to confront Ahab for his rebellion. Elijah challenged the king:

> *"Now summon the people from all over Israel to meet me on Mount Carmel. And bring the four hundred and fifty prophets of Baal and the four hundred prophets of Asherah, who eat at Jezebel's table."* So Ahab sent word throughout all Israel and assembled the prophets on Mount Carmel. (1 Kings 18:19-20)

With righteous indignation, the prophet insisted that Israel no longer waver between two opinions, but choose once and for all who had their full allegiance. The Israelites had nothing to say, so Elijah issued a challenge from the Lord Almighty to the priests of Baal. Elijah insisted:

Get two bulls for us. Let them choose one for themselves, and let them cut it into pieces and put it on the wood but not set fire to it. I will prepare the other bull and put it on the wood but not set fire to it. Then you call on the name of your god, and I will call on the name of the LORD. The god who answers by fire-he is God. (1 Kings 18:23-24)

What followed was a combination of comedy, action, and drama. The priests of Baal frantically prophesied and called on their god to answer by fire while Elijah taunted, *"'Shout louder!' he said. 'Surely he is a god! Perhaps he is deep in thought, or busy, or traveling. Maybe he is sleeping and must be awakened'"* (1 Kings 18:27). One can sense the pleasure of God Almighty through Elijah, as He was about to prove Himself in power far above all gods. The priests of Baal engaged in a frenetic and unsuccessful all-day worship service. Then Elijah upped the ante by requesting that his sacrifice and altar be drenched with water, and a pit be dug around the altar and filled to overflowing. When Elijah called on God, the result was immediate and decisive. The Lord God answered by fire. The priests of Baal were immediately exposed as frauds, and Elijah commanded that they be completely destroyed. A great victory for God was accomplished through the bold faith of Elijah. As a result, the drought was ended, and a heavy rain was brought upon the dry land.

The events on Mount Carmel are a high-watermark for the prophet Elijah. He enjoyed the ultimate "mountaintop experience" that occurred when he challenged the prophets of Baal. It is a pleasure to observe boldness and faith on display in the life of Elijah. In our own day, God is elevating those who, like Elijah, are not intimidated or captivated by the idols of this world, but who are full of faith, power, and an overwhelming joy of spirit that routs the enemies of God.

CHAPTER 18

HOLD ON, PASS IT ON

Keep Your Guard Up

What follows this great victory for God and Elijah at Mount Carmel is an important reminder for us all. We must stay alert in order to preserve our mountaintop experiences with God. After Elijah's conquest over the priests of Baal, we read:

> *Now Ahab told Jezebel everything Elijah had done and how he had killed all the prophets with the sword. So Jezebel sent a messenger to Elijah to say, "May the gods deal with me, be it ever so severely, if by this time tomorrow I do not make your life like that of one of them." Elijah was afraid and ran for his life. When he came to Beersheba in Judah, he left his servant there, while he himself went a day's journey into the desert. He came to a broom tree, sat down under it and prayed that he might die. "I have had enough, Lord," he said. "Take my life; I am no better than my ancestors."* (1 Kings 19:1-4)

Elijah succumbed to fear soon after the greatest victory of his life. He fled from the wicked woman Jezebel and pleaded with God that he might die. What explanation could account for this tremendous shift in spiritual momentum?

Many saints throughout the centuries have experienced a sudden mood shift similar to Elijah's. The truth is that a major spiritual victory such as Elijah's is often followed by a demonic counterattack of fear, intimidation and despair. There is a cunningly waged battle fought by the evil one that is designed to steal back what was taken from his kingdom. An illustration of this comes to mind from our college ministry's annual mission trip to Juarez, Mexico, in the 1990s. Our teams enjoyed a wonderful experience of sharing the gospel, seeing people healed, and being immersed in an environment of faith on these trips. God swept through during the morning worship times, healing and filling hungry hearts while morning teachings gave the students a new perspective on God's kingdom. In the afternoon, the students participated in life-altering outreaches by preaching the gospel to a people who were extremely receptive to God.

One year, the pastor of our hosting church, Daniel Valles, gave an example to our team about preserving what God has accomplished in our lives. He explained that there is a point in a boxing match where the fighter becomes tired and begins to lose energy and focus. As a result, he is tempted to let his guard down by lowering his hands and exposing his chin. If the fighter is not careful, he will find himself lying flat on the mat because his opponent throws a deciding punch that knocks his lights out. Daniel explained that we must be particularly aware to keep on guard against the schemes of the enemy after moments of spiritual victory.

The nature of the evil one must be understood in order to win the fight. Jesus describes that nature by stating, *"The thief comes only to steal and kill and destroy; I have come that they may have life, and have it to the full"* (John 10:10). Satan is a thief, and he will attempt to reverse any gain that advances God's kingdom. However, we can learn to preserve spiritual victories and continue to advance to new heights for God's glory. John Piper explains it this way in his book *Let the Nations Be Glad*: "Life is war. That is not all it is. But it is always that."[23] Awareness of the battle is a key to safeguarding what God has done and pressing on to all that He has in store for us. Fear, unbelief and worldliness are three specific schemes of the enemy we must oppose as fiercely as any foe. Let us consider each of these.

Fear is a primary scheme that the enemy uses against us. Elijah exhibited fear when rebuked by Jezebel and it is a primary area that we must keep up our guard. The enemy is described in the New Testament as a roaring lion (1 Peter 5:8). A lion roars to assert ownership over territory. The roar is meant to intimidate rivals and force animals into submission. "It's mine!" he proclaims. In like manner, Satan instigates fear in our lives in order to intimidate us into allowing him to take what he desires. When we allow fear to rule, we make decisions that are harmful or counterproductive to God's holy will. The mature ones in our midst are those who are not led by the "roar of the lion," but by the voice of the Lamb.[24]

To grow in faith we must walk through fear, not as a one-time process, but as a continual progression. Growing in faith means continually being willing to take a risk in God. An illustration from tennis demonstrates how to overcome fear's grip on our lives in order to walk in greater measures of faith. There is a location on the tennis racquet known as the "sweet spot" that gives great power and precision when the ball is hit correctly. Most amateurs have a difficult time consistently hitting this area, and they deal with a great amount of frustration when the ball careens in the wrong direction. My friend and co-worker in ministry, Jeff Abshire, is a fantastic tennis player, and he is very difficult to beat because he operates in this zone with great consistency. Similarly, we, as believers, are in the sweet spot of God when we choose to be out of our comfort zone. The more often we take God-initiated risks, the more we become familiar with living in the "faith zone" and become devastatingly consistent in defeating the enemy of our souls.

A second scheme that Satan implements is unbelief. After Elijah ran in fear for his life, we see the prophet under a broom tree cloaked in unbelief. Unbelief is often coupled with fear. It is a profound enemy of faith. To break free of the power of un-belief, we must not see it as a character trait or a weakness; but for what it is: sin. The best combatant against unbelief is the Word of God, the Bible, which states, *"So faith comes from hearing, and hearing by the Word of Christ"* (Romans 10:17 - NASB). God's word should be our standard because our feelings can often prove deceptive. John Wimber learned the importance of this truth while preaching through the gospels at the church he founded in Anaheim, California. As he followed the biblical text, he was led to teach on the subject of healing. After several weeks, he grew frustrated because no one got healed. In fact, those who prayed for the sick in his church began to get sick themselves. Many in the congregation left as a result, and Wimber became desperate for an answer to this apparent failure. While in prayer, God spoke a powerful truth to him, "Don't preach your experience - preach my word."[25] After this defining moment in his life, Wimber began to preach God's word, and it became his standard of truth in faith and practice. As a result, God used him to start a healing movement that has impacted millions and invigorated the Body of Christ. Elijah ultimately responded to God and was soon back in the spiritual ballgame. For those who fail to deal with fear and unbelief, however, an additional snare will inevitably result.

Worldliness is a by-product of fear and unbelief. Because the Israelites refused to repent of these sins, their vision was reduced to surviving in the desert instead of conquering the nations before them. They quickly gave in to overindulging in the pleasures of this world. Similarly, fear and unbelief in the Body of Christ lead to a lack of true perspective of God and His purposes on this earth, resulting in worldliness in the Church. If we are not world Christians - believers who have his purposes in view - we will increasingly become worldly Christians – believers focused on this world, rather than on God.

The Great Commission of Jesus Christ was not for a select few people, but for all Christians. We desperately need to understand our part so that we will not, by default, be enamored by worldly pursuits. As in wartime, some are called to go to the frontlines and some are called to stay on the home front, but everyone needs to play his part in the battle. Jimmy Seibert has summarized this in a defining statement for our particular movement, "We are not called to be a church with missionaries, but a church with a mission." When the local body of believers lacks an overall vision for extending the gospel to the ends of the earth, a creeping in of worldliness is inevitable. We should ask God what role He has for us in spreading the Good News to every tribe, tongue, people and language. God will not only answer us, but He will also give each one the power to fulfill His holy purpose.

Passing on the Mantle

A part of God's calling on our lives is to impart what He has given us to the next generation. The first interaction between Elijah and Elisha reads, *"So Elijah went from there and found Elisha son of Shaphat. He was plowing with twelve yoke of oxen and he himself was driving the twelfth pair. Elijah went up and threw his cloak around him. Elisha then left his oxen and ran after Elijah..."* (1 Kings 19:19). A mantle is a symbol of authority. As Elijah threw his cloak upon Elisha, we see the beginning of a transfer of authority to the man who would take the prophet's place. In order to have a mantle to pass on, there are a few important things to consider.

First, we must humble ourselves to receive a spiritual mantle through those who have gone before us in ministry. Humility to receive from others is a deep spiritual lesson we must be aware of and cultivate in our lives. If we have not received, we do not have anything to give. An example of this impartation in my life is in the area of leading worship. Occasionally, after leading worship for a group of people, someone comes up to me to say that they felt a similarity to the singer Keith Green in the way that I worship God. Aside from being completely humbled by this, it is an illustration of impartation from one generation to the next. Though I never met him, Keith Green was my primary leader in praise and worship for many years through his recorded songs. In my desperation and hunger to know God, I would constantly listen to his music in the car and at home. I was transformed by the presence of God while worshipping with Keith, and somehow God imparted to me an ability to produce a similar change in others.

In addition, we should also seek out those who will impart what is lacking in our faith. We are not exempt from daily waiting upon God, but we are also responsible to actively pursue those who are proven and gifted. However, be warned: If you seek the anointing to impress others, it is a dangerous thing. On the other hand, if you desire anointing for the sake of *serving* God and others - "for him and for them" - it is a delightful thing.

In our own movement, I am thankful for leadership that seeks out those who will help us become more effective in loving Jesus and establishing His kingdom. Sometimes we invite experienced people to train us in the subject of evangelism. At other times, we look for those who will further equip us to operate in God's healing power or small group ministry. The particular gift or ministry is not an end in itself, but a means of enhancing our ability to make disciples throughout the world in obedience to the Great Commission.

And finally, we must intentionally pass on our mantles to the next generation. Elijah, even with all of God's power evident in his life, did not wait for his protégé Elisha to come to him. He sought out Elisha and summoned him to receive training and carry on the prophetic ministry. In order to impart what God has given us to the next generation, we, as Elijah did, need to initiate with those whom God has placed in our path. Those who answer His call to full obedience will grow to maturity and become life-long disciples who pass on their investment to the next generation. We should not wait for the next generation to invite us to give them the mantle, or we may look back upon the lost opportunity with regret. My desire to live effectively has motivated me through the years to devote intentional, consistent time with other men for their progress in the faith. Perfection is not required in order to impart life to the next generation. What is necessary is a listening ear, a commitment to prayerful encouragement, and a desire to help them find their "preferred future."[26]

Elijah first initiated with Elisha by going to his village; but as their relationship progressed, it was Elisha who ultimately pursued his predecessor. God was about to take Elijah up in a whirlwind. The Spirit had revealed this to Elisha, and though his master attempted to move on without him on their final journey, Elisha refused to be left behind. This was a divine test to reveal how much of the anointing Elisha truly wanted. The two prophets finally arrived at the Jordan River, and Elijah struck the water with his cloak, parting the water. The account continues, *"When they had crossed, Elijah said to Elisha, 'Tell me, what can I do for you before I am taken from you?' 'Let me inherit a double portion of your spirit,' Elisha replied"* (2 Kings 2:9). Elisha not only wanted the gifts of the Holy Spirit that were in Elijah, but he expected a greater anointing for his life and ministry. When Elijah was taken up to heaven, Elisha kept his eyes fixed on his master, and obtained the "double-portion" he requested.

When Elisha returned alone to the Jordan, the account states:

> *Then he took the cloak that had fallen from him [Elijah] and struck the water with it. "Where now is the Lord, the God of Elijah?" he asked. When he struck the water, it divided to the right and to the left, and he crossed over. The company of the prophets from Jericho, who were watching, said, "The spirit of Elijah is resting on Elisha." And they went to meet him and bowed to the ground before him.* (2 Kings 2:14-15)

God desires that the anointing would increase from one generation to the next. Only a lack of desperation for His divine presence will inhibit such a thing, for God longs to give an increased anointing. It is time for our generation to experience the Spirit of God resting upon it in greater power than any generation before. What this world so desperately needs is the pursuit of the great things of God. He is worthy!

SECTION 10

DANIEL – STAYING POWER

The essential thing in "heaven and earth"
is that there should be a long obedience in the
same direction; there results, and has always resulted
in the long run, something which has made life worth living.
- Friedrich Nietzsche, German Philosopher

When we ring in the New Year, many of us have great
intentions and big dreams for the future. But, be it healthy
living or conscientious driving, most of these resolutions
quickly fade, and our lives return to status quo. Many leaders
in Israel exhibited this lack of commitment in the spiritual
arena and were led astray by their own fleshly appetites.
Standing in clear contrast to these other men, however, was the
prophet Daniel. Having been forcibly relocated to a foreign
land to serve as a teenage, high-level slave, Daniel persevered
through the reign of four pagan kings and influenced the
course of history through the strength of his character.

His unswerving devotion to the Lord and lifestyle of
faithful obedience caused him to finish stronger in godliness
than when he began. John Dawson, President of Youth with a
Mission, observes that in modern society our movies and
popular culture glorify an adulterous spirit. Dawson defines an
adulterous spirit as an attitude that glorifies only the beginning
of relationships.[26] When we buy into the lie that the best is
only what is exciting and new, we tend to grow bored in our
relationship with God and others once the novelty has worn
off. But in actuality, the best relationship is one that maintains
a steadfast commitment through the trials and tribulations of
life in this fallen world. One mature relationship is more
glorious than continually seeking a new one. Because Daniel
walked a "long obedience in the same direction," he is an

inspiration to all who desire to have godly staying power in an adulterous generation.

CHAPTER 19

SEEDS OF RIGHTEOUSNESS

A Godly Heritage

Daniel, a royal son of Judah, was only a teenager when he and his companions faced their first recorded test of godly character. They were forced to decide whether to submit to King Nebuchadnezzar's command to eat food sacrificed to idols, or risk their lives by refusing (Daniel 1:5-16). Imagine the trauma that Daniel first experienced when his family was torn away from their homeland. They had been forced to travel hundreds of miles and were then subjected to slavery in a foreign land due to Judah's rebellion against the Lord. Yet Daniel still chose to abide by the high standards of his God. It is evident that he had a strong godly influence in his formative years who had planted seeds of righteousness in him. Daniel's spiritual commitment as a young man is evidenced as we read, *"But Daniel resolved not to defile himself with the royal food and wine..."* (Daniel 1:8). There is a high probability that someone had spiritually mentored young Daniel, perhaps a parent or another close relative. Godly character does not simply arise out of nothing; it is imparted through purposeful discipleship from one person to another.

My mother, Emma McClendon, was born on June 5, 1940 in Dallas, Texas. She attended Woodrow Wilson High School and met my father during study hall. My parents were married when she was nineteen years old. She gave her life to Jesus in her twenties, and she has been fully devoted to Him since that time. No single person has had a greater influence on my spiritual life than my mother, and those who are privileged to know her can attest to the power of her vibrant faith. From my earliest recollection, she has been full of wholehearted love for Jesus and devoted to prayer. As a child, I would walk into her room and find her beside her bed, kneeling in prayer, with the presence of God filling the room. We cannot overestimate the power of a praying parent or relative in guiding the course of a young person's life. Throughout the years, my mother's desire has been to know Jesus and to make Him known. It was through watching my mother that I learned the ways of God. Just as her influence affected me so profoundly, I can only imagine whom Daniel observed as he learned what it meant to trust in God.

As a result of Daniel's trust in God, he and his three friends who were fellow exiles from Judah exuded holy confidence. They depended on God to grant them wisdom and strength as they abstained from the king's delicacies, which were types of food forbidden by the Law of Moses. When the guard who attended them returned after the days of preparation came to an end, he found them to be "ten times better" than those who ate the royal food (Daniel 1:20). Daniel had learned an important spiritual secret at a young age - wholehearted obedience yields astounding results. In contrast, half-hearted obedience in the church has resulted in mixed results that have been mostly uninspiring to those around us. Daniel knew God, and, as a result he knew the right time and procedure for how to manage what came his way (Ecclesiastes 8:5). The time is now for the church to astound the world; may God show us His perfect way.

Seeing the Unseen

Daniel had a keen sense of eternal perspective. This was another of the righteous seeds planted in him at a young age. One of Daniel's divine functions was that of a prophet, known in Israel at that time as a "seer". He did not judge matters with his physical eyes, but was able to see things as they truly were in the spiritual realm. Centuries later, Paul affirmed the importance of this spiritual perspective by stating, *"So we fix our eyes not on what is seen, but on what is unseen. For what is seen is temporary, but what is unseen is eternal"* (2 Corinthians 4:18). Without being trained to fix our eyes on the unseen, we run the risk of experiencing a crisis of faith. An illustration comes to mind from my wife's home state of Alaska, which is one of the most awe-inspiring places in the world. Due to its size and the mountainous terrain, air travel is a common form of city-to-city transportation in Alaska. When conditions are favorable and the pilot can see clearly, he can fly without relying on his onboard instruments. However, when the weather gets rough and visibility is low, the pilot must depend on his instruments in order to arrive safely. In extreme weather conditions, the pilot runs the risk of becoming disoriented if he depends on his natural senses, and the results can be disastrous. This is a profound example of what can happen in the spiritual realm. By depending on our natural senses in difficult spiritual times, we may become disoriented and the results can be catastrophic.

God longs for a generation of believers who refuse to be ruled by natural sight. He delights in those who choose to see things from His perspective and do not live according to sensuality. Sensuality is not only sexual in nature, but a matter of being governed by our five senses. In order to mature and endure, we must see with our spirit before we see with our natural eyes. Many believers in Jesus make the tragic mistake of relating the blessing of God only to what they feel, touch, and taste in the present moment. The cares of the world attempt to grow as a wild vine in our souls choking out the life of God. A contemporary Christian song expresses the complexity of worldly entanglements in this way:

> *This world has nothing for me*
> *and this world has everything*
> *All that I could want*
> *and nothing that I need.*[27]

How apt these words are for us in this age of complexity. Daniel the "seer" was able to endure and increase in fervor for God to the very end of his life because he chose to "see the unseen." We also need a heightened ability to live according to the unseen realm. When we live according to our five senses, we become disillusioned when things do not happen as we expected; as a result, our devotion to God diminishes. However, this should not be an option for those who are called and chosen by God. We can grow in spiritual strength and zeal until the end of our lives if we repeatedly choose the invisible God as our reward.

The commitment of marriage demonstrates the reward of perseverance that is clearly portrayed in Daniel's life. When my wife Sarah and I were newlyweds, we received a word of encouragement from a vibrant wife and mother of seven children, Janine. She spoke a defining word about marriage by simply announcing, "It only gets better!" We took this as a promise from God that the good, the better, and the best are always ahead of us. My wife and I have needed to remind each other of this truth many times when our five senses were telling us otherwise. From the viewpoint of expecting an ever-growing intimacy in our relationship with God and each other, we have been protected from the temptation toward boredom and bitterness. Like Daniel, we have chosen to live according to the unseen reality of the promise of God. As a result, the seedling of our marriage is becoming an oak of righteousness.

CHAPTER 20

OAK OF RIGHTEOUSNESS

A Man of Holy Influence

Those whom Daniel most influenced by his service were extremely wicked men. We as believers are tempted to become fretful about our nation's leaders when they do not exhibit godly standards. Daniel, on the other hand, did not operate in fear and fretfulness while he served under godless men. The Chaldean despot, Nebuchadnezzar revealed his pagan worldview by proclaiming that Daniel had the "spirit of the holy gods in him" (Daniel 4:9). He also referred to Daniel as the best of his magicians, though the prophet practiced no magic whatsoever. Daniel transformed the worldview of this pagan leader and the kings who followed him not through natural means, but through the power of a righteous life. Nebuchadnezzar, Belshazzar, Darius and Cyrus all eventually acknowledged that the Most High ruled men and nations, and this realization was a result of Daniel's unwavering faith.

Daniel endured an extremely long time of anonymity after the death of Nebuchadnezzar, king of Babylon. His obscurity was evident because King Belshazzar, a descendant of Nebuchadnezzar, needed a reminder from his mother about Daniel and his ability to interpret dreams. Belshazzar had been praising the gods of silver and gold with his friends prior to this, and we read:

> *Suddenly the fingers of a human hand appeared and wrote on the plaster of the wall, near the lampstand in the royal palace. The king watched the hand as it wrote. His face turned pale and he was so frightened that his knees knocked together and his legs gave way.* (Daniel 5:5-6)

It took a terrifying experience like this to bring Daniel out of obscurity. He who had served in the palace during Nebuchadnezzar's reign was nowhere to be seen by the time of Belshazzar. Daniel, however, did not serve God only when he was in the public eye. He was content to love God with his whole being, whether anyone noticed or cared.

When Daniel was brought before Belshazzar, the prophet was completely unimpressed with worldly prizes and possessions. His one pure desire was to please God, and for that reason he lived. Belshazzar offered Daniel the third position in the entire kingdom, to which Daniel replied, *"You may keep your gifts for yourself and give your rewards to someone else. Nevertheless, I will read the writing for the king and tell him what it means"* (Daniel 5:17). Daniel had eternity etched in his mind and knew the truth that the passing pleasures of sin are not worth comparing to heavenly riches (Hebrews 11:25).

Centuries later, William Borden also forsook these passing pleasures for the glory of God. The heir of the Borden Dairy Estate, he was born in 1887 and graduated from high school as a millionaire at the age of 16. For his graduation present, he received a trip around the world from his parents. While traveling the globe, his heart broke for the lost and hurting, and he decided to become a missionary. William wrote two words in the back of his Bible at this time – *No Reserves*. He attended Yale after returning from his worldwide tour and began a morning prayer group during his freshman year. The prayer movement grew to include 1,000 of the 1,300 Yale students by his senior year. Another of his endeavors was the founding of Yale Hope Mission, which reached out to widows, orphans, cripples, and drunkards. William eventually narrowed his focus to reaching the Muslim Kanzu people in China. William received several high paying job offers after graduation, but chose to turn them down. As a result, his father informed him that he was permanently banished from the family business. He then wrote two more words in his Bible – *No Retreats*. William completed his graduate work at Princeton Seminary and sailed to China. While en route, he studied Arabic while living in Egypt. It was there that he contracted spinal meningitis and died at the age of 25. At some point prior to his death Borden wrote another phrase beneath the previous two – *No Regrets.* As with Daniel generations earlier, he was a man who entered heaven with a rich welcome, because he did not seek temporal, earthly riches.[28]

A succession of rulers in Mesopotamia lived for these earthly riches and ruled vast kingdoms. After the Medes and Persians eventually defeated the Babylonians - as prophesied through Daniel - King Darius ascended to the throne. The king and the empire had changed, but faithful Daniel was still ruling in the Spirit. The account of Daniel and the lions' den is a favorite story for young and old alike, and displays the strength of the prophet's character. Daniel was subjected to this severe trial because, once again, he had distinguished himself before the king and become very influential in the kingdom. As a result, other members of the king's staff were jealous of him. Similar to the prophet Samuel, no accusation could be found against Daniel. The only fault his accusers could produce was that he was wholeheartedly committed to God. These envious leaders approached King Darius with flattery and conned him into signing a law stating that no one could worship any god but the king for thirty days. Daniel responded, as usual, in an upright manner. The biblical account states:

> *Now when Daniel knew that the document was signed, he entered his house (now in his roof chamber he had windows open toward Jerusalem); and he continued kneeling on his knees three times a day, praying and giving thanks before his God, as he had been doing previously.* (Daniel 6:10)

And, just as his enemies had anticipated, they spied Daniel praying to his God in defiance of the royal decree. Thom O'leary, Lead Pastor of Mountainview Community Church in San Luis Obispo, once referred to this as "getting caught being faithful." Daniel was not a spiritual chameleon who adapted his appearance to the environment in which he lived; he was a lifelong worshipper of God. He was "caught" for the right reason. He had developed a habit of gazing at the Faithful One, and as a result, that is what Daniel became - faithful.

When Daniel was thrown into the lions' den, the devious leaders were convinced that they had won an overwhelming victory. The law of the Medes and Persians refused to allow the king to change his mind, so he was powerless to alter the decree after he discovered the true intention of the schemers. It appeared that Daniel's life would certainly be extinguished and these hateful men would triumph. Quite often, this is how it appears with God's servants. In fact, this was how it appeared when Jesus was crucified. Every demon in hell rejoiced because He had been slain. But "*Sunday's coming*" as Reverend E. V. Hill proclaimed:

> The religious leaders mocked Jesus while he was on the cross.
> *It's Friday - They didn't know that Sunday's coming.*
>
> Herod toyed with the Lord, but when Jesus wouldn't play along, Herod sold the Lord down the river. Herod mocked Jesus.
> *It's Friday, but Sunday's coming!*
>
> The crowds shouted, "Crucify him! Crucify him! Crucify him!" – Jesus was crucified.
> *It's Friday, but Sunday's coming.*

Pilate thought he could wash his hands of the whole thing.
It's Friday – but, hey governor - Sunday's coming!

The soldiers beat Jesus and spat on him and pushed a crown of thorns on his head.
It's Friday - They didn't know that Sunday's coming!

Satan and his minions jeered and shouted with glee on that dark Friday. They must've missed the prophecies;
It's Friday. Sunday's coming!

And death, that enemy that has hunted humanity down for countless generations, death must've thought if he could just take this Jesus Christ down into the grave and hold Him; but death, you messed up, cause,
it's only Friday. Sunday's coming!

Well - Sunday's here, and the grave is empty! Not the religious leaders, not Herod, not Pilate, not the blood-thirsty crowd crying 'crucify him', not the soldiers, not Satan –and especially not death - could hold Jesus in the grave![29]

After a sleepless night, King Darius ran to the lions' den, and he found God's man alive. Daniel had trusted in God, and as a result he was not disappointed. We can see the magnitude of this miracle as we read:

> *At the king's command, the men who had falsely accused Daniel were brought in and*

thrown into the lions' den, along with their wives and children. And before they reached the floor of the den, the lions overpowered them and crushed all their bones. (Daniel 6:24)

These beasts were ravenous and only the almighty power of God could have kept their mouths shut throughout the night. The glory of God was promoted in the kingdom of the Medes and Persians as a result of Daniel's faith. The severe test produced a glorious testimony of God's triumph. Tests and testimony always go together. Jimmy Seibert once stated, "Everyone wants a testimony, but few people are willing to go through what it takes to get one." The life of Daniel was a testimony of God's grace and power because Daniel did not give way to fear and intimidation. Similarly, the Lord had challenged another Judean prophet not to submit to the fears common to man:

Do not call conspiracy everything that these people call conspiracy; do not fear what they fear, and do not dread it. The Lord Almighty is the one you are to regard as holy, he is the one you are to fear, he is the one you are to dread... (Isaiah 8:12-13)

Daniel had such a revelation of God's preeminence that he did not waver before rival allegiances. He feared God above all else, and as a result he changed the course of nations.

CHAPTER 21

PRAYER AND PROPHECY

Twentieth Century American evangelist Billy Sunday stated, "If you are a stranger to prayer, you are a stranger to the greatest power known to human beings."[30] Daniel lived a life of prevailing prayer that allowed God's power to be displayed through him on a continual basis. His intimacy with God resulted in extraordinary influence with people. Daniel received prophetic revelation from God because he delighted to live daily in the shadow of God's presence. The Psalmist says, *"The LORD confides in those who fear him; he makes his covenant known to them"* (Psalm 25:14). Daniel feared the Lord, and the Lord confided in him and was pleased to reveal divine secrets to this prayerful listener. He was not only a God-fearer; he was a God-lover. Daniel's love for God was extravagant, and he lives on as an example of one who was rich toward God in all of his ways.

Jay Livingston and Ray Evans wrote the memorable theme song of the *Doris Day Show* (1968-1973), entitled "Que Sera Sera". The chorus goes:

> *Que Sera, Sera,*
> *Whatever will be, will be*
> *The future's not ours, to see*
> *Que Sera, Sera*
> *What will be, will be.*[31]

In contrast to this worldly from of fatalism, Daniel remained confident that his prayers would change the course of history. He persisted as a man of prayer throughout his life, and remained faithful to God in his later years while serving under King Darius. Having realized that the desolation of Jerusalem would last seventy years, grief overwhelmed Daniel, and he was compelled to pray. We read: *"So I turned to the LORD God and pleaded with him in prayer and petition, in fasting, and in sackcloth and ashes"* (Daniel 9:3). When we examine these words, several aspects of mountain-moving prayer emerge. These include identification, confession, petition and perseverance. Accompanied by the practice of fasting, these can prove to be a powerful and effective means of bringing heaven to earth.

The first detail we observe in this passage is that Daniel identified with his people. As evidenced by our study thus far, Daniel lived above reproach in his personal life and had an impressive track record of obedience to God. However, when he began to pray for the Israelites, he did not smugly separate himself from his people, but said, *"I prayed to the Lord my God and confessed...we have sinned and done wrong. We have been wicked and have rebelled; we have turned away from your commands and laws"* (Daniel 9:4-5, emphasis mine). Humility is a requirement for true intercession, and identification is an outworking of humility. Rather than an attitude of superiority that judged his fellow Israelites, Daniel brought them before God by identifying with his people and their sin.

Another element of prayer that is highlighted for us in this passage is confession. Daniel simply admits, *"Now, O LORD our God, who brought your people out of Egypt with a mighty hand and who made for yourself a name that endures to this day, we have sinned, we have done wrong"*(Daniel 9:15). True biblical confession calls sin what it is and does not make excuses for it. God longs to forgive, but He only forgives those who quit defending themselves by trying to prove that their sinful actions are justifiable. Confession is not based solely on a feeling, but on the reality of our offense before God. Some individuals only confess at the level of their actions, but it is necessary to ask God to search our hearts for the attitudes that lead to sinful actions. Sin occurs through a process of faulty thinking that promotes sinful attitudes and ultimately progresses to sinful actions. When we go to the root of wrong thinking in our confession, we will begin to see the fruit of a righteous life in our actions.

As we continue to consider Daniel's prayer, we see faith operating through bold petition. Petition is defined as making a definite request of God. The intercessor and prophet Daniel pleads, "*O LORD, listen! O LORD, forgive! O LORD, hear and act! For your sake, O my God, do not delay, because your city and your people bear your Name*" (Daniel 9:19). True petition like this is clear and concise. In contrast, Jesus rebuked the Pharisees because they thought they would be heard for their many words. When we pray with vague and wordy prayers, we demonstrate that we don't know what we truly want. Children in need of something are very clear about the object of their desire. God intends for us as His children to petition Him in specific ways in order to obtain from Him what we need. Remaining in God's word enables us to make our requests known with great precision and with assurance that He hears and will surely answer. A sign of a spiritually mature person is one who knows God's will and prays specifically in order to see it brought to pass.

Finally, by examining Daniel's life, we also see the vital necessity of perseverance.

The prophet continues:

> *While I was speaking and praying, confessing my sin and the sin of my people Israel and making my request to the LORD my God for his holy hill- while I was still in prayer, Gabriel, the man I had seen in the earlier vision, came to me in swift flight about the time of the evening sacrifice. He instructed me and said to me, "Daniel, I have now come to give you insight and understanding. As soon as you began to pray, an answer was given, which I have come to tell you, for you are highly esteemed. Therefore, consider the message and understand the vision."* (Daniel 9:20-23)

We gain true perspective from this passage about why we must persevere until we receive our answer from God. The angel Gabriel explained to Daniel that as soon as he began to pray an answer had been given. However, the archangel did not appear until three weeks after Daniel began praying. This was due to intense spiritual warfare in the heavenly realms (Daniel 10:12-13). We should be greatly encouraged by this illustration in that, the answer is immediately on the way when we ask according to God's will. Some answers come instantaneously, while others face resistance from the enemy for a time. But as surely as the sun rises, the answer will come through perseverance in prayer.

The delightful Suzette Hattingh, co-founder of Voice in the City and former head of intercession for Reinhardt Bonnke Ministries, gave a poignant illustration of the need for perseverance in prayer. Suzette shared about an instance that occurred while she was driving in Germany years ago. While cruising along, she realized that she must have missed a turn, because the road came to a sudden end. She made an abrupt stop to avoid an accident, and, while peering out at the unfinished road, the Lord spoke to her heart. He said, "Suzette, this is what your prayer life looks like. You have started many roads in prayer, but after time you have quit building in these areas. Your prayer life is filled with half-built highways."[32] Suzette shared that she immediately repented and picked up where she had left off in these prayer projects until she saw what she was asking God for with her own eyes. Likewise, when Jesus instructs us on prayer in the Sermon on the Mount in Matthew 7, He uses the "present imperative" verb for the words "ask," "seek," and "knock." In other words, He challenges us to "ask and keep on asking," "seek and keep on seeking," and "knock and keep on knocking." Our faith in prayer can be buoyed by the knowledge that He hears us and the answer is on the way from the first moment we ask.

A Stored Up Inheritance

Daniel was effective during *his* life because he was living for the *next* life. He was entrusted with power and prominence in the land of Babylon because he did not seek honor for himself. God desires for us to be successful, but not at the expense of His glory. When we are committed to God's fame, He may give us favor with men, but for His sake. In the last verse of Daniel's story, an angel says to him, *"As for you, go your way till the end. You will rest, and then at the end of your days you will arise to receive your allotted inheritance"* (Daniel 12:13). Daniel honored God for decades and served a succession of kings with complete integrity. He was about to receive that which God had stored up for him. This is reminiscent of David's declaration, *"How great is your goodness, which you have stored up for those who fear you, which you bestow in the sight of men on those who take refuge in you"* (Psalm 31:19). Our God is storing up goodness for those who fear Him, and none can repay like Him. When we live our lives as Daniel did, with enthusiasm for our eternal King, we will walk in strength and increase in faith to the end of our days.

SECTION 11

PETER - A SECOND CHANCE

*You may have a fresh start any moment
you choose, for this thing we call 'failure' is
not the falling down, but the staying down.*
- Mary Pickford, Co-Founder of United Artists

The Apostle Peter was a dynamic figure throughout the Gospels, and a significant player in the book of Acts. He was the key figure immediately after the ascension of Jesus and was used to establish the church in Jerusalem. In addition, he was instrumental in changing the viewpoint of the church toward the Gentiles through a vision he received at Simon the Tanner's home. This vision and Peter's subsequent visit to Cornelius' house revealed that all men were included in the plan of God for redemption through the Gospel of Christ. Introduced to the Lord Jesus by his brother Andrew, Peter was immediately affirmed by Jesus regarding God's mighty purpose for his life. Cephas' name was changed to Peter, translated as "rock," when Jesus stated, *"And I tell you that you are Peter and on this rock I will build my church, and the gates of Hades will not overcome it"* (Matthew 16:18). Even as Jesus spoke to Peter about his destiny, He was fully aware of the young fisherman's inconsistency and impetuousness. Peter still needed to learn about God's ways and his own weakness in order to be prepared to fulfill these promises of God.

Peter was a work in progress. Initially, he had a highly inflated opinion of himself. But after years of God's loving discipline, he instead exuded a confidence that came from a high view of God. By the time the apostles gathered in Jerusalem following the ascension of Jesus, Peter was not impressed with his own gifts and accomplishments. He was in awe of the great God of men and God's ability to use weak and defective people to accomplish great things. Peter started out

159

full of self-strength and dependent on his own abilities. Yet, when the Lord was fully glorified in him, Peter credited God for all that had been done. He had learned through bitter experience that the man God uses must be broken of the self-life and dependent on God alone. This is the way of the Lord Jesus, who stated, *"I tell you the truth, the Son can do nothing by himself; he can do only what he sees his Father doing, because whatever the Father does the Son also does"* (John 5:19). It took years for Peter to fully incorporate Christ's example of dependency into his own life, but by the end, he had learned his lesson well. The same Peter who denied Jesus three times was eventually crucified upside-down because he did not consider himself worthy to die in the same way as his Lord.

Impulsive Peter was in the thick of the action throughout the Gospels. Using modern day lingo, we would call him a "motor mouth." In one instance he called Jesus *"the Christ"* (Matthew16:16-17) showing insight from God, yet soon thereafter, Jesus strongly rebuked him with, *"Get behind me, Satan!"* (Matthew 16:23), because Peter tried to convince Jesus not to go to the cross (Matthew 16:23). On the Mount of Transfiguration, Peter spoke impetuously and was silenced by the Father's voice from heaven. Following Christ's prediction that the disciples would all fall away from Him, Peter declared, *"Even if I have to die with you, I will never disown you"* (Matthew 26:35). And in addition to his zealous words, Peter picked up a sword in the Garden of Gethsemane and cut off the slave Malchus' ear (John 18:10). At that time, Jesus was obliged to remind him that the true nature of the battle with the hordes of hell is spiritual, not earthly. Finally, just hours later, Peter stared into the eyes of his Lord after having denied Him three times (Luke 22:61). Jesus had called him, loved him, and believed in him; yet, during the Lord's greatest hour of need, Peter's best efforts fell woefully short. Peter came face to face with the fact that human zeal is a tragically poor substitute for holy dependence.

CHAPTER 22

THERE IS A REDEEMER

Through observing Peter's life we see a clear depiction of Jesus' unending patience with those who choose to pursue Him. The Lord took Peter's mistakes and redeemed them because Peter was quick to repent and follow again. A description of Jesus' high priestly ministry is found in the book of Hebrews, which states, *"Therefore he is able to save completely those who come to God through him, because he always lives to intercede for them"* (Hebrews 7:25). Picture the Son of God, our Savior, calling out to the Father on our behalf, "Father, they have failed again, but they are repentant; work this together for good. Bring all of the enemy's schemes to ruin!" Our Advocate has destroyed our accuser and He is on our side.

Through my friend, Greg Riggs, I experienced a living example of the continual prayers of Jesus for my welfare. It was during my teenage years that I became friends with Greg. He began attending our church's youth group and came to know Jesus as his Lord and Savior soon thereafter. When he surrendered to Christ, he was completely given to God and was a consistent man of integrity and faith. In contrast, I began to drift from my relationship with God and eventually found myself given to ever-increasing rebellion. We both attended the same university, and since I was playing the prodigal, Greg and I drifted apart. His purity of life was a strong rebuke to my worldliness during that season, and I preferred to avoid any reminder of my condition. When I returned to Jesus my junior year, however, Greg was one of the first people I wanted to see. I walked across campus to his dorm room and shared with him the amazing work that God had done in my life. While I was there, I happened to notice a sheet of paper on his desk. It was his prayer list. My name was written there! He had been calling out to God for my life at the very time I had needed it the most. My heart was filled with thankfulness for Greg's loving friendship, and I stood in awe of Jesus, who always intercedes for me.

Jesus is for us, but Satan is the accuser of the brethren, and he revels in foul play. When someone is down, he delights to kick him; if someone is upbeat, Satan tries to deceive him. A basic scheme of our enemy is to get our eyes off of God and onto ourselves. The Psalmist proclaims, *"My eyes are ever on the LORD, for only he will release my feet from the snare"* (Psalm 25:15). We are challenged in this verse not to stare at the snare of being preoccupied with our sin, our shortcomings, or ourselves. Peter would never have been able to recover from his heinous denial had he not looked into Jesus' eyes and received His mercy. Peter had a deep and abiding revelation that his sin and shame were nothing compared to his Lord's astounding love and forgiveness. Obtaining the freedom we so desperately need comes not by looking inward, but by gazing at the Righteous One.

While a lack of heartfelt conviction about our sin surely leads to destruction, an obsession with our sin leads to spiritual paralysis. We need a greater revelation that whatever causes us to think obsessively about ourselves is not from God. The Apostle John encourages us, *"But we know that when he appears, we shall be like him, for we shall see him as he is"* (1 John 3:2). We resemble that which we look at, so the best response to this reality is always to look at the Lord. When we refuse Satan's accusations and listen to the affirming voice of our heavenly Father, our faith in God grows exponentially.

In addition, Peter's life is a clear portrayal of God's delight in giving a second chance and working out a new "best" for those who repent and turn to Him. An Old Testament example of God's redemptive best can be observed in His dealings with the tribe of Levi. Levi was the third born of Jacob (also known as Israel), and son of his favored wife Rachel. A tragic series of events began when Shechem, of a nearby tribe, raped Dinah, the sister of Levi. We read, *"When Shechem son of Hamor the Hivite, the ruler of that area, saw her (Dinah), he took her and violated her"* (Genesis 34:2). God surely would have judged this vile act, but Levi and his brother Simeon, taking matters into their own hands, resorted to a vengeful ruse. They assured the Hivites that the Israelites would intermarry with their tribe if every male were circumcised. Shechem's father Hamor agreed, and the entire tribe was circumcised. The biblical account continues:

> *Three days later, while all of them were still in pain, two of Jacob's sons, Simeon and Levi, Dinah's brothers, took their swords and attacked the unsuspecting city, killing every male. They put Hamor and his son Shechem to the sword and took Dinah from Shechem's house and left.* (Genesis 34:25-26)

As a consequence of this ruthless act, Simeon and Levi received a curse from their father at the end of his life. Jacob said to them, *"Simeon and Levi are brothers, their swords are weapons of violence...I will scatter them in Jacob and disperse them in Israel"* (Genesis 49:5, 7). Centuries later, when the Promised Land was parceled out, neither of these men's descendants would possess their inheritance in the same way as their brothers. Simeon's descendants lived in towns dispersed throughout the area of Judah, confined within his younger brother's inheritance. Levi's descendants were scattered throughout all eleven of the other tribes of Israel. However, Levi's story includes an encouraging example of the redemption of God.

Redemption can be defined as God establishing a new "best" for his children when they have strayed from his commands. In the example of Levi, when Moses had come down from the mountain after receiving the Ten Commandments, he discovered that some of the people had corrupted their worship through unbridled idolatry. As a result, God's wrath was on the Israelites, and Moses ordered them to strap on swords and kill the rebellious ones. The Levites quickly obeyed and killed three thousand Israelites in obedience to the Lord's command. As a result, Moses said to the Levites, *"You have been set apart to the LORD today, for you were against your own sons and brothers, and he has blessed you this day"* (Genesis 32:29). Though judgment was upon the nation of Israel due to the rebellion in their midst, God chose this opportunity to use the Levites to establish His holiness and turn their longstanding curse into a blessing. They had been scattered in Israel as a result of their ancestor's disobedience, but they were now set apart throughout the tribes as priests of God. From that day forward, instead of land, the Lord was their portion in Israel. This is a wonderful testimony of God's ability to turn our sin and blunders into blessings if we will repent and give our whole hearts to Him. Our Judge has become our Redeemer. He is righteous in His judgment but prefers to extend forgiveness and a fresh start to those who turn to Him.

CHAPTER 23

GOD OF SECOND CHANCES

The Valley of the Shadow of Death

At a most unwelcome and unexpected time in my life, I was brought back to the very foundation of my relationship with God, even to the point of questioning God's intentions toward me. Just as with Simon Peter, Satan had asked to sift me like wheat, but Jesus my Lord stood by my side and prayed for me that my faith would not fail (Luke 22:31-32). For the seven years prior to this crisis, I had been leading discipleship training schools from our local church to locations across the globe. We preached the gospel, planted churches, and believed for nations to be transformed. There was, however, an increasingly legalistic approach to my spiritual life, and I was about to pay a high price for this attitude. While I prayed, fasted, and preached, much of what I was doing was not based out of a center of who God had made me to be. I developed a competitive spirit in my spiritual life - working hard to outdo others through spiritual performance. My identity became more wrapped up in doing spiritual things than in being a truly spiritual man as God had intended. Accepting the praise of men, I became convinced that I was a great man of God. But He allowed me, by His grace and lovingkindness, to realize that He is truly the great God of men.

In the spring of 1997, after years of equipping others for the mission field, I led a church planting team to Berlin. As we left Texas for Germany, I was filled with great confidence that I was fully qualified to plant a dynamic, nation-changing church. Having prepared people to plant churches, evangelized and challenged people to walk in a lifestyle of faith, I felt that I was fully prepared for any challenge. As with Peter, generations earlier, my spirit seemed to say, *"Even if all fall away, I will not"* (Mark 14:29). What I failed to see around the bend was that God would allow an experience that tested my five senses to the furthest extent. After a few weeks in Berlin, I began to experience some difficulty with my eyesight and thought that something was wrong with my vision. After explaining these symptoms to friends, I visited an ophthalmologist. Test results came back negative; it was not an eye problem.

Soon after realizing that my eyes were okay, the first signs of depression began to set in. Although I still worshipped, prayed, and called out to God, symptoms much worse than failing eyesight overtook me. What at first seemed simply a mild case of "having a bad day" became a suffocating cloak of darkness surrounding me; the feelings eventually drove me to a major emotional breakdown. As I began to realize that there was no easy way out of this darkness, I found myself giving up on life. My identity had been formed by others' opinions of me, and when I realized that I was failing these expectations, an utter hopelessness pressed on my heart like a vice. Due to my complete inability to continue the work, Jimmy Seibert, the president of our missions organization, flew to Europe to bring me back to Texas. A few days later I was admitted to a psychiatric hospital. The words of John Wesley, the father of Methodism, spoke loud and clear to my situation at that time. While on his way back to England from Georgia after experiencing bitter failure, he wrote:

> *I went to America to convert the Indians; but O! Who shall convert me? Who, what is he that shall deliver me from this evil heart of unbelief? I have a fair summer religion. I can talk well; nay, and believe myself while no danger is near; but let death look me in the face and my spirit is troubled...O who will deliver me from this fear of death?*[33]

My wonderful team supported me through this unexpected turn of events, and I will forever be grateful to them for their love and patience. However, no matter how much they tried to encourage me to the contrary, I was convinced that I had absolutely failed God, and I was overwhelmed with despair. The future was as dark as midnight, and I could not comprehend how I had erred so dreadfully to be punished in this way. Filled with dread, my mind began working against me, and the devil did not play fair in my time of trouble. Though I had completely given up on life and welcomed the thought of death, God had not relinquished His grip on me. Even though I slept for almost twenty-four hours a day - even though I could do nothing for God - He held vigil over me.

It was much like another watch that God held over me when I was a small, defenseless newborn. An Rh-negative blood condition developed into yellow jaundice, and pushed my infant body to the verge of death soon after my first breath of life. My initial hours on earth consisted of five blood transfusions and an anxious wait for my mom and dad. The attending doctor warned my parents not to expect me to live, but they, in faith and desperation, gathered a group of friends to pray. A more accurate explanation is that Jesus gathered them to pray, and through their prayers He healed me. In the same way that I was helpless physically without the intervention of God at the beginning of my life, I came to realize during this time of depression in adulthood that I was just as helpless emotionally without His mighty hand.

After being discharged from the hospital following my return from Germany, I survived one minute at a time. Eventually, I was able to handle life hourly, and then daily, but no answers from God appeared for many months. As the years passed, however, I gained valuable perspective on this time in my life: What seems like cruelty for the moment can often be kindness for a lifetime. Although the psychological pain was intolerable, God protected me with His kindness from remaining in despair and from returning to anxiously performing for Him and for people. He prepared me to live the rest of my life with greater love and peace than I had ever known. A scripture

I had learned prior to the whole crisis said it best: *"My flesh and my heart may fail, but God is the strength of my heart and my portion forever"* (Psalm 73:26). My flesh and heart had truly failed, but God was my strength even when I could not perform. "Failure" in this situation did more for me than success could ever have done. Rather than allow me to run from the fear of failure that tainted everything I did, God caused me to face it head on and set me free from the bondage of perfectionism. Though I had failed, I was not a failure as long as I moved forward every step with God. Through the lovingkindness of my friends and family in the Body of Christ, I started down a path of restoration and began to experience greater fullness and security than I had ever known. It is a joy to know that I am now walking on ground the devil didn't want me to walk on, and every step is to the glory of God.

For a short period of time, Peter also must have been convinced that God had given up on him. But he came to know that for those in the valley of despair, Jesus' power to hold us is more than our power to let go of Him. How could Peter make it up to God for denying Him so completely? The sobering truth is that he could not have made it up in a million years. He had arrived at the moment in his life when he could not make things right, no matter how hard he tried. Peter's failure was going to be broadcast through the Gospels for the rest of history. There was no way to disguise this and no way to hide from it. And this was precisely the place that Jesus wanted him, completely dependent upon the mercy and grace of God. Whatever happened from this time forward would be credited to God and God alone. No more could Peter take credit for anything good coming from his life. He would move forward in life and ministry with amazement that God would use a person such as him. Peter would no longer have the attitude, "God is blessed to have me," but rather, he would carry the realization that he was blessed to be a part of God's plan. He would gladly play any role God desired as long as the Lord was the one glorified through it.

Restored for a Purpose

Following Jesus' resurrection from the dead, He reinstated Peter and assured him of His love. The Lord was not only content with forgiving Peter, but He lavished His love on this dear friend. The first way that Jesus affirmed Peter was in the garden outside of the tomb. He told the women to whom He had appeared to tell the disciples *"and Peter"* that He had been raised from the dead (Mark 16:7). Jesus specifically mentioned Peter, as if to say, "All is forgiven." In addition, before Jesus ascended to the Father, He asked Peter to reaffirm his love for Him three times. The Lord made sure that Peter was able to confess his love once for each time that he had denied Him. These two interactions reveal that our Lord is more concerned with our wholeness and restoration than we are, and He will not rest until He completes His holy work in our lives.

In the remainder of the New Testament, save one instance (Galatians 2:11), Peter is a completely new man. When we see him in the first book of Acts, he is decisive in the matter of finding a new apostle to replace Judas. Peter was free from condemnation, and everything that he was missing on the night of Jesus' betrayal was suddenly there: boldness, compassion, and the fear of the Lord. On the day of Pentecost, he proclaimed, *"Therefore let all Israel be assured of this: God has made this Jesus, whom you crucified, both Lord and Christ"* (Acts 2:36). Peter was no longer a politically correct man who cowered in fear at the slightest threat, but a man full of the Holy Spirit and the fear of God. He knew that he had nothing to lose; he had the love and forgiveness of God. The Apostle Peter had been given a second chance.

SECTION 12

JOHN THE BELOVED - INTIMACY

To fall in love with God is the greatest of all romances;
to seek him, the greatest adventure; to find him,
the greatest human achievement.
- St Augustine, Bishop of Hippo

Those who know God personally receive revelation from Him. The apostle John was our Lord's most intimate friend on earth and as a result, he was entrusted with the words that became the New Testament's prophetic book, the Revelation of Jesus Christ. John was so intimate with the Lord that even Peter, at the Passover table, asked him to inquire of Jesus as to who would betray Him. John, this "Son of Thunder," knew God through the person of Jesus and experienced His love in a profound way. He even described himself in the gospel that he penned as *"the disciple whom Jesus loved"* (John 13:23 – KJV). John was also entrusted with the responsibility of caring for Jesus' mother at the time of the Lord's death. This honor and responsibility bestowed upon John by our Redeemer testifies to the depth of their relationship. It was this closer-than-family quality of relationship with Jesus that drove John the Beloved throughout his life and ministry. John's depth of friendship with Jesus is a worthy example for us to follow.

James and John, the sons of Zebedee, were fishing partners with Peter and Andrew's family. The moment that Jesus called these men to Himself, they left their nets and followed without hesitation. John zealously accepted the call to discipleship and desired to be with his master no matter the cost. The gospels of Matthew, Mark and Luke, also known as the synoptic gospels, are similar in content. They contain the overriding theme of the kingdom of God through a relatively similar series of messages, actions, and miracles. John's gospel, however, is written from a unique perspective - that of John remembering his friend and Savior as fully divine and eternal. In the latter

171

part of his gospel, John chose to highlight a prayer of Jesus where the Lord declared, *"This is eternal life: that they may know you, the one true God and Jesus Christ whom you have sent"* (John 17:3). John was determined, through the particular selection and order of what he wrote, to specifically convey that we were not only saved from death and destruction, but we were brought into an eternal, benevolent relationship with God and with His Son Jesus. John was enamored with the person of Jesus and his gospel conveys a detailed view of the multi-faceted love of God from the unique perspective of being the Lord's best friend.

CHAPTER 24

DO NOT LOVE THE WORLD

Title and rank are highly valued by mankind, but, more than any of these accolades, John desired to be near his Lord. Those who are primarily concerned about their position among people are, by default, not situated closely enough to Jesus. In contrast, when we strive with God for the place of intimacy with Him, we will find ourselves striving less with others. John drew near to God, and from that place of strength, he was well equipped to love those around him.

John loved others enough to communicate very directly about the true nature of love. He urged and warned them to live their lives worthy of God. One of John's exhortations made a deep impact on me several years ago when a roommate of mine, Craig, wanted to more firmly establish a morning routine of seeking Jesus. Around 6:00 every morning, I would knock on his door with a Bible in one hand and a pot of coffee in the other, and we would give ourselves to God first thing in the morning. As we sought God, we were impressed with a scripture written by John the Beloved that states:

> *Do not love the world or anything in the world. If anyone loves the world, the love of the Father is not in him. For everything in the world - the cravings of sinful man, the lust of his eyes and the boasting of what he has and does - comes not from the Father but from the world. The world and its desires pass away, but the man who does the will of God lives forever.* (1 John 2:15-17)

John unequivocally states in this passage that the man who loves this present world does not possess the love of the eternal Father. He mentions three worldly attitudes that are in direct opposition to love for God. As we consider these, we can gain more perspective on how to love God.

The first ungodly attitude that John mentions in this passage is the cravings of sinful man. Webster defines a "craving" as an intense, urgent, or abnormal desire or longing. In the New American Standard version of the Bible, these cravings are called, *"the lust of the flesh"* (1 John 2:15 – NASB). God gives bodily desires to us, but they have become swollen and abnormal through the distorting nature of sin. Although Satan did not create our desires, he twists them in order to gain dominion in our lives. We, as followers of Jesus, must be ruthless toward the sinful cravings that war against our souls. These cravings certainly include, but are not limited to, the sexual realm. The eye is indeed the window to the soul, and we must guard what we watch with vigilance to protect our hearts. This watchful victory happens, however, by renewing our minds with the truth, not by waiting on life to become free of temptation. To illustrate, on a summer day in Boston a number of years ago, I was riding on the "T" (the city's public transportation). There were a number of scantily clad women aboard. A thought came to me, *"Boy, I can't wait for winter to get here,"* but immediately the firm voice of God pressed my mind, *"Jeff, winter is not your deliverance, I am."* This is a vital key to sexual freedom. We cannot blame our circumstances for sexual temptation; it is an internal renewal that we need. To wait for externals to change before we can be free of sin is foolishness.

For whatever new trial or temptation our society man-ufactures, there is a greater grace from God to overcome it. There are no limits to the freedom from sin that we can enjoy if we do not tire of humbling our hearts before God and men. However, we must deal as radically with sin as Jesus instructs:

> *If your hand causes you to sin, cut it off. It is*
> *better for you to enter life maimed than with*
> *two hands to go into hell, where the fire never*

> *goes out. And if your foot causes you to sin,*
> *cut it off. It is better for you to enter life*
> *crippled than to have two feet and be thrown*
> *into hell. And if your eye causes you to sin,*
> *pluck it out. It is better for you to enter the*
> *kingdom of God with one eye than to have two*
> *eyes and be thrown into hell.* (Mark 9:43-47)

Too many times, we treat temptation like a calico cat that we pet from time to time until it bites our ear off. We tolerate sin because somewhere inside, we do not truly hate it. But on the contrary, we need to treat sin as a mangy dog coming into our house. When we ask God for a holy hatred of sin, borne out of a passion for God, He will gladly fill us with His holy desires. It is time to attack sin with all of our might, resist it, and sentence it to the death that it deserves. When we begin to hate sin, we are starting to love God as He truly deserves.

Another ungodly attitude that John addresses in this passage is the lust of the eyes, also known as covetousness. Few people are truly content with who they are and what God has given them. James, a brother and fellow apostle of John, states:

> *What causes fights and quarrels among you?*
> *Don't they come from your desires that battle*
> *within you? You want something but don't get*
> *it. You kill and covet, but you cannot have*
> *what you want. You quarrel and fight. You do*
> *not have, because you do not ask God.* (James
> 4:1-2)

The lust of the eyes pertains to envy or desiring what you see at the expense of another person. Left unchecked, these unholy longings result in fights, quarrels and ultimately, murderous thoughts and actions. If we fail to deal ruthlessly with the sin of covetousness in our lives, it will persist in enslaving us. Repentance is the only true doorway to freedom from this determined foe. But we can only repent of what we recognize is wrong in the first place. Jimmy Seibert has shared on numerous occasions: "If you can't call it sin, you can't get rid of it." In Ephesians 3, Paul puts covetousness on the same level as the sins of idolatry and adultery. We should not hide or make excuses for the lust of the eyes, but call it what it is, and God will release us from its firm grip.

Training our spirits toward thankfulness is a weapon that slays the enemy of covetousness and discontentment. By practicing a grateful attitude, we are enabled to live with contentment in our daily lives. Years ago, a friend of mine was going through an extremely difficult relationship breakup, yet daily she had a joyous outlook on life. One day I asked her how she was walking with such strength in the midst of the trial. She explained that she did not get out of bed in the morning until she had thanked God for at least ten things. She chose not to wrap herself with the tempting cloak of self-pity and discontentment, but fought the good fight with a thankful heart. She is an unforgettable example to me of one who has battled covetousness and overcome. Until we deal with the issues of covetousness and discontentment, we are unable to appreciate the season that God has given us. Eternal perspective is vital to living a victorious life because when we fail to meditate on the benefits of the King and His kingdom, we will revert to the factory settings of humanity that are rooted in comparison and jealousy, the ingredients of covetousness and discontentment.

The final ungodly attitude that John addresses is the boasting of what we have and do. Those who are not secure in God will feel the need to impress men. Blatant displays of this attitude abound in our affluent culture with opulent cars, mansions, and gaudy jewelry. Our modern media validates a worldly appetite for possessions and accomplishment. Simplicity is the antithesis of boasting in what we have and do. For example, when considering employment or possessions, we would do well to ask two questions in order to avoid the snare of unholy boasting. The first question to consider is whether a job or possession will increase or decrease our ability to love Jesus. A second consideration is to determine whether this action will improve our effectiveness in seeing sinners saved and believers built up. When my wife and I make a decision regarding a major purchase, the first two questions we try to ask ourselves are, "are we willing to allow this object to be freely used by others if God so desires?" and "will this possession add spiritual value to our community of faith and the city we live in?" By not loving the world, as John exhorts us, we are able to love the people in this world as God truly intended.

CHAPTER 25

TRUE LOVE

One of my favorite movies is the comedy classic *Princess Bride* (1987). In this movie, Princess Buttercup is forcibly engaged to marry the selfish Prince Humperdinck, but she actually has another true love, Westley. The man of her dreams comes to her rescue just as she and the dreadful prince stand before a priest at a hurriedly performed marriage ceremony. The priest begins the marriage with a sermon in a comical lisp, about "Wuv, twue wuv" (love true love). Westley rescues Buttercup and she is reunited with her true prince charming. What, however, is "true love" from God's perspective?

John equates our love for the God who is unseen with the quality of love we express to people whom we can see. He exhorts, *"If anyone says 'I love God, but yet hates his brother, he is a liar and the truth is not in him'"* (1 John 4:20). What a clear challenge for us to repent of pretense and live by God's holy standard! An insecure and unloving person - one who does not have the truth of God's love in him - is one who demands to win an argument at another's expense. Paul Billhiemer, in his book, *Love Covers,* warns about this kind of argumentative spirit, naming it an attitude of "rightness" that is opposed to authentic love. He challenges:

> No breach in the Body of Christ is ever caused primarily by superior knowledge, differing convictions, or divergent views of truth; but by one thing and only one - lack of agape love. Therefore, the only remedy will be found in growth of love, that is, authentic love for God. Mark this well: In any controversy over nonessentials, the question is not primarily who is right; not even who is most nearly right. The real question is: Is there sufficient

maturity in the love of God to cover differences in nonessentials and unite the Body?[34]

The goal of the Christian life is not to be right, but to
overcome evil with God's love. Stubbornness and unforgive-
ness create a spiritual wall between people, often starting with
one specific disagreement. Sometimes the wall can even be a
literal one. Salvatore and James Dell'Orto, for example, owned
two adjacent stores by the names of Manganaro Foods and
Manganaro's Hero Boy. After a dispute, these brothers spent
decades working on opposite sides of a common wall two
bricks thick without so much as a word between them. These
blood relatives did not have a conversation for twenty-five
years. What was the insurmountable issue? It was the question
of which store had the right to take telephone orders for party-
size sandwiches - the Hero-Boy - under the Manganaro name,
a name inherited from the brothers' uncle, who took over the
original store.[35] This true story illustrates the tragic
consequences of a stubborn and unforgiving spirit.

Some churches have split over reasons that are just as
trifling to the outside observer. Divisions and disputes based
on a need to be proven "right" dishonor God and destroy men.
Our goal as believers should not be to set everyone straight in
the miniscule details of their doctrine, but to preserve unity
and reveal Christ through the way we love one another in spite
of our differences. This attitude of true love will enable us to
aim our spiritual guns at the forces of darkness instead of one
another, and in the words of evangelist Reinhardt Bonnke, we
will hear the Holy Spirit say to us, "You will plunder hell to
populate heaven, for Calvary's sake!"[36]

We Want to See Jesus

John's Gospel describes a group of Greeks who came to
worship at the Passover Feast. They approached Phillip with
this request, *"'Sir,' they said, 'we would like to see Jesus'"*

(John 12:21b). This desire to "see Jesus" was the express intent of John the Beloved from the moment he came to know the Lord and minister in His name. Toward the end of his life, John was exiled to the island of Patmos, but received a jaw-dropping vision that became the book of Revelation. It is not primarily a revelation of the end times, but the revelation of a person, Jesus Christ. This vision was given to John – by that time over 90 years old. At the beginning of this revelation, John turned to see the voice speaking to him and saw the glorified Jesus standing among the seven golden lamp stands (Revelation 1:12-16). John, likely the Lord's closest human companion, one who was more familiar with Him than anyone on earth, was nevertheless completely undone and fell at the Lord's feet like a dead man. This scene gives clear evidence that Jesus far surpasses our most vivid dreams or wildest imaginations.

John was eventually released from Patmos, and died, according to church tradition, from old age under the care of the church at Ephesus. He received a rich welcome to his eternal home. John, an alien on earth because of his devotion to Christ, finally found his true country. An American folk narrative may help us understand how we, as Christians walking in the legacy of John, await arrival in our true home:

> An old missionary couple had been working in Africa for years and were returning to New York to retire. They had no pension; their health was broken; they were defeated, discouraged, and afraid. They discovered they were booked on the same ship as President Teddy Roosevelt, who was returning from one of his big-game hunting expeditions.
>
> No one paid any attention to them. They watched the fanfare that accompanied the President's entourage, with passengers trying to catch a glimpse of the great man.

As the ship moved across the ocean, the old missionary said to his wife, "Something is wrong. Why should we have given our lives in faithful service for God in Africa all these many years and have no one care a thing about us? Here this man comes back from a hunting trip and everybody makes much over him, but nobody gives two hoots about us."

"Dear, you shouldn't feel that way," his wife said.

"I can't help it; it doesn't seem right."

When the ship docked in New York, a band was waiting to greet the President.

The mayor and other dignitaries were there. The papers were full of the President's arrival, but no one noticed this missionary couple. They slipped off the ship and found a cheap flat on the East Side, hoping the next day to see what they could do to make a living in the city.

That night the man's spirit broke. He said to his wife, "I can't take this; God is not treating us fairly."

His wife replied, "Why don't you go in the bedroom and tell that to the Lord?"

A short time later he came out from the bedroom, but now his face was completely different. His wife asked, "Dear, what happened?"

"The Lord settled it with me," he said. "I told him how bitter I was that the President should receive this tremendous homecoming, when no one met us as we returned home. And when I finished, it seemed as though the Lord put his hand on my shoulder and simply said, 'But you're not home yet![37]

The apostle John was distinguished by a love for God and His eternal kingdom. If our love does not distinguish us from those who love the world, we must stop and consider for which kingdom we are really living. Keith Green, in the spirit of that same heavenly expectation, sang these words shortly before his death:

> When I stand in glory
> I will seek his face
> And there I'll serve my king forever
> In that holy place.[38]

May we live as John the Beloved did, loving in such a way that speeds Jesus' return to earth.

SECTION 13

BARNABAS - THE POWER
OF HOLY INFLUENCE

*Those who lead the church are marked by a willingness
to give up personal preferences, to surrender legitimate
and natural desires for the sake of God...the true
leader is concerned primarily with the welfare of
others, not with his own comfort or prestige.
- Oswald Sanders, Spiritual Leadership*

What is it that defines true greatness? Is it money, possessions, fame, or a position of authority? Successful business-
men, politicians, athletes, and actors are considered great in the
eyes of the world, but upon closer inspection, many do not
hold up to the standard of true greatness. So what, then, is it?
A few years ago, I awoke suddenly during the night with my
heart pounding in my chest and a compelling thought pressing
on my mind, "My dad is a great man." Although songwriting
was familiar to me, I had never written a poem until that
moment. As I wrote, it began to crystallize in my mind that
true greatness is vastly different than what the spirit of this age
would suggest. The following is the poem that I penned for my
father, Ted Bianchi, that night:

You're a Great Man

*As life goes on and things come up that put me to the test,
These are the things about you, dad, that stand above the rest.
You always made me feel, dad, so special in your eyes.
I never thought you cared for work more than your "Little Guy."
You taught me of integrity, what you say, you do.
While other men where cheating, to my mother you stayed true.
You've been a great provider, in word as well as deed.
Thank you dad for going without, so I'd have all I need.
You taught me how to be a man who's loyal to the bone.*

When others run, you stick it out, that's all I've ever known.
When people ask, "How do you define greatness in a man?"
I'll tell them of the one who raised me to be the one I am.

Dad's greatness was that he considered his wife and children as more important than himself. This influence still lives in me and through me produces an influence upon others.

God has put a desire in the human heart to make a mark on history - in essence, to affect, even change, the world. The desire to be great and to conquer has obsessed men from such vastly different locations and cultures as Napoleon of France to Genghis Khan of Mongolia. Mike Bickle explains that one cannot repent of the desire to be great, but of attempting to be great for the wrong reasons.[39] We have a divinely implanted longing for God's greatness to be manifest through our lives, but unholy ambition occurs when that God-given desire is twisted, and we begin to covet reputation - glory - for ourselves.

Human beings were initially designed by God to exert a holy influence upon other people and ultimately the entire creation. This is evidenced by God's command for Adam and Eve to multiply and rule the earth (Genesis 1:28). Due to original sin, however, the nature of our influence suddenly changed from God-exalting and peace-promoting to man-exalting and often destructive. As humans made in God's image, we cannot help but have an influence upon others. The pertinent question is whether we will be influencing people toward God or not. Only those who grow in humility and freedom from selfish ambition will have a lasting godly impact. In addition, our private lives - personal devotion to God as well as secret sin - affects other people because it affects the nature of our influence. True godly influence was depicted in the life of John the Baptist when, upon seeing Jesus, he announced to his disciples John the Beloved and Andrew, *"Look, the Lamb of God"* (John 1:36)! Andrew immediately called his brother Peter, and these two disciples began to follow Jesus. When asked later about Jesus' growing ministry, John the Baptist replied, *"He must become greater; I must become less"* (John 3:30). In like manner, Barnabas was one who influenced many for righteousness. As we reflect upon his life, may we grow in our desire and ability to exert holy influence and change the course of many lives.

CHAPTER 26

LOOK UP, LOOK OUT

Eyes on Eternity

Barnabas was fully devoted to Jesus and a champion for the cause of the poor. Luke introduced him by stating, *"Joseph, a Levite from Cyprus, whom the apostles called Barnabas (which means Son of Encouragement), sold a field he owned and brought the money and put it at the apostles' feet"* (Acts 4:36-37). While many people of his day were building their own kingdoms and tending to their own businesses, Barnabas was concerned about building the kingdom of God. He possessed an eternal heavenly perspective, which may have come from hearing these words while in Jesus' presence:

> *Store not up for yourselves, treasures on earth where moth and rust destroy and were thieves break in and steal, but store up for yourselves treasures in heaven where moth and rust do not destroy and where thieves do not break in and steal, for where your treasure is, there will your heart be also.* (Matthew 6:19-20)

Men of godly ambition and eternal perspective have made their mark throughout history and have left an example for us to follow. Years ago, Jimmy Seibert and I had the privilege of going to a prayer meeting in East Texas attended by one such man, Leonard Ravenhill. He had authored books such as, *Why Revival Tarries* and was a continual advocate for God's reviving work in His people. It was an awe-inspiring experience seeing this elderly prophet on his knees before God and knowing that the prayers of this righteous man were accomplishing a great deal in the heavenly realm. Leonard Ravenhill's soul burned with the fire of God until his last breath because he continually lived with eternity before him. In the words of the late Mr. Ravenhill:

> *When Jesus was condemned... they put an old, dirty robe on him and he wore that stinking robe that you might wear a robe of righteousness. How often do you think of that? They put a crown of thorns on his head that you and I might wear an eternal crown. He was separated from the Father that we might be brought to the Father. He took on human nature that we might have divine nature. He left eternity for 33 years so we could go to eternity for 33 billion years...*[40]

Another man obsessed with eternity was Arthur Stace, an Australian who gave his life to Christ in 1930 after a life of petty crime and alcoholism. In 1932, he heard his pastor exclaim that he wanted to shout "Eternity!" through the streets of Sydney. In response, Stace determined to make this a reality. After an hour with the Lord each morning, he would leave his home between 5:00 and 5:30 a.m. and anonymously write one word, "Eternity", approximately every 100 feet on the sidewalks of Sydney. He did this for a total of thirty-five years and it is estimated that he wrote this word 500,000 times. This one-word sermon caused thousands to pause and consider their lives. In 1956, the identity of the mystery man was discovered. Following his death in 1967, a copper plate in honor of Stace with the word, "ETERNITY", was put in Sydney Square. Later, during the opening ceremony of the 2000 Sydney Olympics, over four billion people worldwide viewed this plate.[41] Like Barnabas, Stace lived for eternity and, as a result, led a selfless, consistent and fruitful life that touched the nations of the earth.

Son of Encouragement

Barnabas' name means "Son of Encouragement," which is an accurate description of how he gave courage to others and empowered them to overcome. He epitomized the scripture that says, *"But encourage one another daily, as long as it is called Today, so that none of you may be hardened by sin's deceitfulness"* (Hebrews 3:13). We as followers of Christ are responsible to protect one another from deception through the ministry of encouragement. Life in this sinful world can cause genuine, faith-filled believers to become hardened to God's word, which results in deception. The news media and prevailing public sentiment do not encourage us to follow Jesus, but instead attempt to reinforce a worldly mindset. In contrast, we who are filled with God's Spirit have power to speak words and perform actions that soften other's hearts to the living God.

Joe Ewen, a dear friend and mentor of mine, has lived out this Barnabas-style ministry for many years. He was a fisherman on the north shore of Scotland for seventeen years when Jesus apprehended him in a radical way. Similar to Peter, Andrew, James and John, Joe gave up his fishing boat to become a leader of church planting and renewal. He developed a close friendship with Jimmy Seibert in the late 1980s following an outreach that Jimmy led to Scotland. While I ministered with Jimmy during my formative years of ministry in Texas, Joe would often call at what seemed to be the perfect time with life-giving encouragement. These words were tailor-made for that exact moment and deeply encouraged Jimmy and our young movement. During an international conference for our missionaries in 2006, Joe was awarded a twenty-five year ministry plaque in recognition of his tireless leadership and service to our movement. Many people were in the room representing young churches scattered throughout the world. Jimmy asked them, "If you have had a significant word given to you from Joe that has deeply affected you and encouraged your call to overseas missions, please stand up." Eighty to ninety percent of the people in the room stood up to testify of the encouragement that God had given them through this Scottish prophet. Joe's life is a living definition of the term, "Son of Encouragement."

Spiritual Talent Scout

Barnabas recognized the potential in Saul, the future Apostle Paul, in spite of the way he was viewed by others. Barnabas saw Saul's godly destiny and helped him to achieve it. We read:

> When he [Saul] came to Jerusalem, he tried to join the disciples, but they were all afraid of him, not believing that he really was a disciple. But Barnabas took him and brought him to the apostles. He told them how Saul on his journey had seen the Lord and that the Lord had spoken to him, and how in Damascus he had preached fearlessly in the name of Jesus. So Saul stayed with them and moved about freely in Jerusalem, speaking boldly in the name of the Lord. (Acts 9:26-28)

Barnabas, contrary to the apprehension and suspicion of the other believers, sought out Saul, who had spent three years in Arabia growing in Christ (Galatians 1:17-18). Barnabas convinced church leaders that Paul's faith was genuine. He took a risk so the gospel message could be furthered and God's name would be honored. God's glory was of greater concern to him than his own reputation and comfort.

Although he defended Paul to the Jewish Christians in Jerusalem, Barnabas eventually came into sharp dispute with Paul, whom he had earlier defended to the Jews in Damascus. The disagreement arose because Barnabas saw potential in his young cousin John Mark, even though the young man had abandoned Paul and Barnabas on an earlier missionary outreach (Acts 14:36-40). The "Son of Encouragement" was unwilling to give up on him and saw something redeemable in John Mark's life and ministry. We do not know the exact conversation that ensued between these two men, but Barnabas, Paul's mentor, likely could have said, "Hey Paul, do you remember Damascus, when I believed in you and no one else did? Why don't you get off your high horse and take a chance on this young one; he deserves another chance."

At that time, however, Paul could not be convinced, and the biblical account states, *"They had such a sharp disagreement that they parted company. Barnabas took (John) Mark and sailed for Cyprus, but Paul chose Silas and left, commended by the brothers to the grace of the Lord"* (Acts 15:39-40). Barnabas' spiritual intuition was eventually proved right about John Mark, and Paul later requested that John Mark be brought to him because he was helpful in the ministry (2 Timothy 4:11). Barnabas did not see people through the lens of the past, but through the prophetic lens of the future. He was under divine inspiration to see who they could ultimately become.

As an avid fan of college football, I have observed two main factors that are necessary in order for a coaching staff to succeed in this sport. One of these factors is to locate and acquire talent, and another is to be able to develop that talent to its maximum potential. We, as disciples of Jesus, are called to do this as well. More than simply looking for talent like the world does, we are to look for a heart after God. When God sent Samuel to Jesse's house to anoint the new king of Israel, Samuel expected the impressive firstborn of Jesse's family to be the chosen ruler. However, the account says:

> But the LORD said to
> Samuel, *"Do not consider his appearance or
> his height, for I have rejected him. The*

LORD does not look at the things man looks at. Man looks at the outward appearance, but the LORD looks at the heart." (1 Samuel 16:7)

We should ask God to give us supernatural vision to see clearly whom the Lord is anointing and then boldly call those people out to the destiny God has for them. As Barnabas demonstrated in working alongside Paul, we ought to develop these people through life coaching to become all they can be in God.

Barnabas possessed a revelation of the redeeming power of God and the ability of the Holy Spirit to change people's lives. He had a lifestyle of calling people to greater things in God than they could have ever imagined. Those who are spiritually mature must see things as they are going to be, not dwell on things as they are. The writer of Hebrews exhorts, *"Now faith is being sure of what we hope for and certain of what we do not see"* (Hebrews 11:1). We are commissioned to lead those whom God has placed in our lives into a future for which they are longing, but do not know how to reach without spiritual guidance and holy encouragement. Barnabas helped many others achieve their potential and shared in the joy of seeing them flourish. We would do well to follow his lead and expect God's power to miraculously change lives.

The Power of Holy Influence

Barnabas was such a powerful mentor because he was willing to simply play his role. He gave his all so that others would reach their full potential. Paul echoed this attitude that he saw in Barnabas when he stated:

> *We do not dare to classify ourselves or compare ourselves with some who commend themselves. When they measure themselves by themselves and compare themselves with*

themselves, they are not wise. We, however, will not boast beyond proper limits, but will confine our boasting to the field God had assigned to us, a field that reaches even to you. (2 Corinthians 10:12-13)

When I began in ministry, I was more concerned about title and position than I cared to admit. I was offended when I felt that I was not getting the recognition that I deserved. Out of insecurity and immaturity, I had the mistaken impression that position automatically meant influence. However, as the years have gone by, titles have become less important. What matters more than ever to me is to influence others regardless of my position. For I have found that when we covet a position, we lose influence in that area. But as we accept the role that God has given us to play and give ourselves to it wholeheartedly, we increase in godly influence. As a result, the Lord will be able to promote us as He sees fit.

Henrietta Mears, a twentieth century Barnabas, exerted great influence simply by working in the field to which she was assigned. She was born in Fargo, North Dakota, in 1890, and was so nearsighted that she thought she might be blind by age 30. However, she was sure that God had a wonderful purpose for her life. She read and memorized all that she could in case her eyesight failed. In 1928, Mears became the director of education at Hollywood Presbyterian Church in California. Soon after attending the church, she began to develop Bible curriculum that she used to mentor youth toward a deeper faith in Christ. Through the labors of this single woman, God influenced two of the most instrumental Christian leaders of the twentieth century: the evangelist Billy Graham and Bill Bright, founder of Campus Crusade for Christ. She also led the actress and singer, Dale Evans Rogers to the Lord. In the forward to the book, *The Henrietta Mears Story,* Billy Graham writes:

...She has had remarkable influence, both directly and indirectly, on my life. In fact, I doubt if any other woman outside of my wife and mother has had such a marked influence. Her gracious spirit, her devotional life, her steadfastness for the simple gospel, and her knowledge of the Bible have been a continual inspiration and amazement to me. She is certainly one of the greatest Christians I have ever known!

As a result of this woman's obedience, literally millions of people's lives have been changed for the glory of God through the ministries of those she influenced.

God is looking for a generation who find their calling through helping others to become all they can be in God. In an age of self-seeking and vainglory, there is a fragrance from self-denial that is a pleasing fragrance to God. Peter admonished us, *"Each one should use whatever gift he has received to serve others, faithfully administering God's grace in its various forms"* (1 Peter 4:10). It will require a daily habit of saying no to selfish ambition and worldly living. May we take hold of the attitude exemplified by Barnabas, the Son of Encouragement, who desired one thing above all else, the glory of God.

SECTION 14

PAUL – HOLY AMBITION

Some men's ambition is art,
Some men's ambition is fame,
Some men's ambition is gold,
My ambition is the souls of men.
- Written by General William Booth
in King Edward VII's autograph book

Where would the church of Jesus Christ be today without the loving labor of the apostle Paul? God used this man of faith to establish the fledgling church throughout the Roman Empire in an astonishingly short period of time. He also provided a doctrinal foundation that has served the church of Jesus Christ up to the present day. Paul's life personified the words of Jim Elliot, missionary martyr to the Auca Indians of Ecuador, who once stated in a journal entry from *Shadow of the Almighty*: "Father, make of me a crisis man. Bring those I contact to decision. Let me not be a milepost on a single road; make me a fork, that men must turn one way or another on facing Christ in me."[43]

Paul had trained as a Pharisee under the tutelage of Gamaliel, an elder who was a leading authority in the Sanhedrin in the mid first-century. Paul – called, "Paullus" in the Roman world, and "Saul" in Jewish circles - was a zealous and diligent man, but he was not yet God's man. Paul's zeal masked a secret desire for recognition in the eyes of men. The process of maturity for this Pharisee was found in the shift from seeking his own glory to seeking the glory of God. By pursuing our own glory, we hurt people; but by pursuing God's glory we heal people. Paul witnessed and approved of the death of Stephen (Acts 8:1), and later went to believers' houses to forcibly remove them and imprison them in Jerusalem (Acts 9:1-2). He was completely earnest in his intention to destroy the church, thinking God was on his side,

197

but his path was unknowingly set against God Almighty. He was in for a rude awakening that would dramatically change the course of his entire life.

CHAPTER 27

SHARING IN HIS SUFFERINGS

While traveling on the road to Damascus to persecute the church in that city, Paul came face to face with the resurrected Christ. We read:

> *As he neared Damascus on his journey, suddenly a light from heaven flashed around him. He fell to the ground and heard a voice say to him, "Saul, Saul, why do you persecute me?" "Who are you, Lord?" Saul asked. "I am Jesus, whom you are persecuting," he replied. "Now get up and go into the city, and you will be told what you must do." The men traveling with Saul stood there speechless; they heard the sound but did not see anyone. Saul got up from the ground, but when he opened his eyes he could see nothing. So they led him by the hand into Damascus. For three days he was blind, and did not eat or drink anything.* (Acts 9:3-9)

Paul's encounter with Jesus provides us with some valuable insights about our Lord. It would benefit us greatly to consider them.

Jesus apprehended Paul while appearing on the road to Damascus. "Apprehend" is a violent word that means to take by force. A great many devoted people view God as a gentleman who would not interfere with someone's life unless they wanted Him to. Though it is true that God will not ultimately override our will, He will apprehend those who are called and chosen, often through the prayers of the saints, giving them a clear opportunity to submit to Christ's lordship. For example, while I played the prodigal in my late teens, the fervent prayers of my family and friends sought me out and found me with a wonderful and fearful apprehending. After four years of reckless living, the Lord Jesus, through the presence of the Holy Spirit, entered the bedroom of my college apartment. He revealed to me in no uncertain terms that He had first claim on my life, and that my time of worldly living was up. In response to God's intervention, I surrendered all of me to all of Him for the rest of my life. Jesus does not beg us to come to Him - He calls us to follow Him and commands complete obedience. Abundant knowledge of God's loving-kindness coupled with a healthy dose of the fear of the Lord will enable us to prosper spiritually for the long haul.

As we look at the Lord's confrontation of Paul on the road to Damascus, we gain insight into Jesus' intimate relationship with us - His body. To Jesus, the persecution of Christians is a persecution of Himself. While the bright light was shining on Paul, Jesus did not ask, *"Why are you persecuting my people?"* but *"Why are you persecuting me?"* We are one with Him in every way, and when we experience suffering, He suffers as well. This reality should greatly comfort us when are going through times of trial for our faith. While exhorting the believers in Philippi, Paul declared, *"I want to know Christ and the power of his resurrection and the fellowship of sharing in his sufferings, becoming like him in his death, and so, somehow, to attain to the resurrection from the dead"* (Philippians 3:10-11). Toward the beginning of my relationship with Jesus, I greatly appreciated the first half of this scripture, but not the second half. However, after years of experiencing His faithfulness, I have a growing desire to share in either suffering or resurrection, as long as it is with Him.

People who have endured similar hardships often develop a deeper bond with each other than those who have not had a comparable experience. The story of one family's hardship is an example of this. My wife and I are honored to be friends of two sisters, Lia and Sonia, who attend our church in Boston. They and their husbands have been like family to us as we have shared our lives together. These women lost their father,

Elia, in the Pan AM Flight 103 bombing over Scotland in 1988. Lia, Sonia and their mother, Mary Kay, meet yearly with those whose family members perished in this tragedy, and they have developed a deep bond of shared experience. These people share each other's pain, offer comfort to one another, and seek ways to honor their lost family members. Mary Kay, who suffered the loss of her husband in the bombing, has led an effort to bring comfort and guidance to families who lost loved ones in the 9/11 terrorist attacks. She is able to comfort effectively because she herself has passed through the "valley of the shadow of death" (Psalm 23:4) with her Lord.

Similarly, those who suffer for Christ often experience God's presence in a way that is deeper and fuller than those who have not suffered for Him. When we endure hardship for the sake of Jesus, there is a camaraderie with Him that cannot be explained to the casual observer. Christ's presence simply becomes sweeter in the context of suffering. My friends Dayna (Curry) Masterson and Heather (Mercer) al Khoury experienced this truth firsthand. We traveled together to Afghanistan in 1998, when they decided to move to Kabul in order to serve the orphans and widows of that city. In 2001, they were imprisoned for their faith. For over three months a host of believers from many nations joined in prayer on their behalf. The world eventually rejoiced at their release after 104 days in captivity. While speaking with these ladies after their imprisonment, an overriding theme that struck me was their description of the nearness of Jesus to them during that time. To my surprise, Dayna commented that during her hectic speaking tour after her miraculous release, she actually *missed* being in prison because the presence of God was so sweet in that place. Those who have suffered for the sake of the gospel possess a radically different perspective than that of our popular Christian culture. Both of these women are still serving Muslims and are committed to seeing the gospel of the kingdom preached to all nations. Their lives shine as examples of what is meant by "the fellowship of sharing in His sufferings" (Phillipians 3:10).

CHAPTER 28

SUCCESSFUL CHURCH PLANTING

A Sense of Urgency

Immediately following Paul's blinding encounter with Jesus, God told a believer in the city of Damascus named Ananias to place his hands on Paul so he would receive back his sight. When Ananias met Paul for the first time, Ananias exhibited resolute faith by announcing, *"Brother Saul, the Lord--Jesus, who appeared to you on the road as you were coming here--has sent me so that you may see again and be filled with the Holy Spirit"* (Acts 9:17). Ananias called him "brother," even though this man had determined to do Christians harm just days earlier. Why? Because Ananias intently listened to and obeyed God. He was a faithful man whom God used as an instrument to release one of the greatest influencers the church of Jesus Christ has ever known. We never hear of Ananias again in the biblical narrative, but his profound legacy continues to this day through the man who became known as "The Apostle to the Gentiles."

Following Paul's conversion, he wasted no time in proclaiming Christ as Lord. We read, *"At once he began to preach in the synagogues that Jesus is the Son of God"* (Acts 9:20). Paul was so successful in confounding the Jews and persuading them to believe in Christ that the persecutor soon became the persecuted. He was forced to escape his opponents by leaving Damascus under the cover of night. From that moment on, Paul knew he had a relatively short period of time to complete the mission God had entrusted to him. He lived with a sense of urgency as he fulfilled his responsibility of making Christ known to the Gentiles. We see his determination displayed as he spoke to the Ephesian elders in Miletus. He declared, *"However, I consider my life worth nothing to me, if only I may finish the race and complete the task the Lord Jesus has given me--the task of testifying to the gospel of God's* grace" (Acts 20:24) Paul lived with a burning zeal to see churches planted throughout the entire Roman world before he died.

D.L. Moody had an experience on Sunday, October 8, 1871, that changed his outlook on the urgency of his divine mandate for the remainder of his life. While preaching that night at the YMCA's Farwell Hall in Chicago, Moody asked his congregation to evaluate their relationship with Christ and return the next week to make their decisions for Him. That crowd never gathered again. While Ira Sankey was singing a closing song, the din of fire trucks and church bells evoked panic in the listeners: the Great Chicago Fire had begun. The Y.M.C.A., churches, and virtually every building in 3.3 square miles were lost in the next twenty-four hours. More than 90,000 were left homeless; the crowd at Farwell Hall was scattered forever. D.L. Moody never again waited until the next day or week to call people to a decision to follow Christ because, like Paul, he had learned the urgency of preaching the gospel.[44]

An Unrelenting Resolve

Paul was successful in preaching the gospel and planting churches because he possessed a heavenly mindset and an unrelenting resolve. Paul was single-minded in his mission from God, and he would not be deterred from it. There was incredible power in Paul's ministry because he gave all he had for the souls of men and the establishing of the church. The apostle knew what his mission was and he gave all of his energy toward that one goal. We ought to heed the writer of Hebrews when he says, *"Therefore, since we are surrounded by such a great cloud of witnesses, let us throw off everything that hinders and the sin that so easily entangles, and let us run with perseverance the race marked out for us"* (Hebrews 12:1). Sin and worldliness entangle us and prevent us from living in a focused manner. We should take our bearings from men and women of faith throughout the generations who have placed their energy into one supreme purpose. Their example can enable us to steer clear of useless pursuits and live in an effective way for God's kingdom.

A Holy (Spirit) Expectation

Paul also made widespread impact because he operated in faith that the Holy Spirit would profoundly change the communities he visited. A simple definition of the word faith is "expectation". Paul expected that the gospel of Jesus Christ would shake the world, and he functioned in ministry with this mindset. In the book *Missionary Methods: St Paul's or Ours,* Roland Allen rebukes those who had drifted away from such a mindset. He states, "Just scattering seed hoping with a vague hope that some of it will come up is not preaching of the Gospel of Christ."[45] To the Corinthians, Paul also wrote:

> *When I came to you, brothers, I did not come with eloquence or superior wisdom as I proclaimed to you the testimony about God. For I resolved to know nothing while I was with you except Jesus Christ and him crucified. I came to you in weakness and fear, and with much trembling. My message and my preaching were not with wise and persuasive words, but with a demonstration of the Spirit's power, so that your faith might not rest on men's wisdom, but on God's power.* (1 Corinthians 2:1-5)

Those who depend on clever speech rather than faith are hindered in their ability to proclaim God's message with power. Paul was utterly determined not to attempt to win the world by the world's wisdom; he did not rely on intellect, but determined to focus on the message of salvation through

Christ, trusting that in this way the Spirit would confirm his message. This faith-filled adherence to the simple gospel invited the miraculous power of God.

God did not intend for signs and wonders to be a stage production that makes Christian meetings better. As much as I appreciate how God touches and heals Christians because of His love for them, the main role of the supernatural is to open doors to people who have been previously closed to the gospel. This is the example of the New Testament accounts of miracles. Signs and wonders are not optional in the proclaiming of the gospel to the unreached, but are a vital necessity. Many of the arguments in our Western institutions that dispute signs and wonders prove to be folly when we take the gospel to the uttermost parts of the world. It is in those places, where few belong to Christ, that we begin to understand that no mere human technique will deliver men from darkness. Deliverance is obtained by preaching the gospel of the kingdom with power. People who desire to see God's power should preach the gospel to the unreached. It is in that environment that the supernatural often overtakes our words and opens hearts.

While in Indonesia with one of our outreach teams in 2009, we experienced the power of God that opened doors for the gospel. We had arrived in Surabaya, the second largest city in Indonesia, with a desire to see people saved and a movement of God started. After a couple of days of preaching in the city and seeing limited results, we felt that there was more that God wanted to do. We waited on God for direction during our morning prayer time, and we felt impressed that He was leading us to an area on the northwest side of the city near an island where no known indigenous churches existed at that time. A group from our team went to one of the enclaves in the city called a *kampung*. We moved down the main street and a member of our team, Amy, asked people to bring out their sick for healing prayer. An elderly man came and invited me to his home, where he and several people were healed of various sicknesses. The atmosphere of faith was tangible, and we knew as we prayed that God was touching these people with His divine healing power.

The next day, we arrived at the same kampung, and a woman immediately came up to us explaining that she had heard of the healings the previous day, but had been working at that time. She invited us into her home and asked us to pray for her to be healed of a condition causing pain and numbness in her arm. We explained to her that only Jesus can heal, and we placed our hands on her in His name. The look on her face said it all - she had been healed! She moved her arm freely with great joy. After we prayed for her friend and saw her healed too, it resulted in an open door to preach the gospel. The woman and her friend received Christ, and they asked us to return to teach them more about Jesus. We sang a song of rejoicing, and the woman with the healed arm went onto the street beaming with God's love and testifying with a dance in her step to what the Lord had done for her.

It greatly concerns me that we in the Western church try to imitate worldly methods in the hope of winning people to Christ. We should not want to be popular; rather, we should want to be effective in winning people to Jesus. In evangelized regions, we often play games and look for strategies that do not necessarily require the presence of God to get results. But when we are advancing into new territory, these games and tricks will not work. Paul chided the Corinthian church for its worldliness, saying, *"The kingdom of God is not a matter of talk, but of power"* (1 Corinthians 4:20). If we are to accomplish God's will in our generation, we must have the power of God as Paul did when he preached the gospel throughout the Roman world. When Jesus is all that we have, He is all that is needed.

CHAPTER 29

UNCHARTED TERRITORY

In the late 1800's, Meriwether Lewis and William Clark eagerly desired to explore uncharted territory in the United States. Their endeavor took two years, four months and ten days, and covered 8,000 miles. They were not content with the status quo. President Thomas Jefferson commissioned them to open up the wilderness for America's future growth.[46] Likewise, Paul possessed a holy desire to press into uncharted territory for God's kingdom, and he trusted the Holy Spirit to work in people's lives to mature what he had planted. Paul did not view his mission as creating perfect churches, but as creating movements of people. He knew that he was called to be an apostle, and therefore he did not get tied down with long pastoral assignments. He handed churches over in an expedient way to allow those gifted as pastors and teachers to flourish in each Christian community he started. Then he would move on. He explained to the believers in Rome, *"It has always been my ambition to preach the gospel where Christ was not known, so that I would not be building on someone else's foundation"* (Romans 15:20). In 1979, James M. Weber, a missionary to Japan, wrote a parable illustrating the mindset that must be overcome in order to recapture Paul's apostolic zeal for un-reached people. Here is the parable as it appeared in the 1979 printing of *Let's Quit Kidding Ourselves About Missions*:

Orchard Parable:
The Society for the Picking of Apples

Once upon a time there was an apple grower who had acres and acres of apple trees. In all, he had 10,000 acres of apple orchards. One day he went to the nearby town. There, he hired 1,000 apple pickers. He told them: "Go to my orchards. Harvest the ripe apples, and build storage buildings for them so that they will not spoil. I need to be gone for a while, but I will provide all you will need to complete the task. When I return, I will reward you for your work." I'll set up a Society for the Picking of Apples. The Society -- to which you will all belong -- will be responsible for the entire operation. Naturally, in addition to those of you doing the actual harvesting, some will carry supplies, others will care for the physical needs of the group, and still others will have administrative responsibilities."

As he set up the Society structure, some people volunteered to be pickers and others to be packers. Others put their skills to work as truck drivers, cooks, accountants, storehouse builders, apple inspectors and even administrators. Every one of his workers could, of course, have picked apples. In the end, however, only 100 of the 1,000 employees wound up as full-time pickers. The 100 pickers started harvesting immediately. Ninety-four of them began picking around the homestead. The remaining six looked out toward the horizon. They decided to head out to the far-away orchards. Before long, the storehouses in the 800 acres immediately surrounding the homestead had been filled by the 94 pickers with beautiful, delicious apples.

The orchards on the 800 acres around the homestead had thousands of apple trees. But with almost all of the pickers concentrating on them, those trees were soon picked nearly bare. In fact, the ninety-four apple pickers working around the homestead began having difficulty finding trees that had not been

REFLECTIONS ON THE PATH TO SPIRITUAL MATURITY

picked. As the apple picking slowed down around the homestead, Society members began channeling effort into building larger storehouses and developing better equipment for picking and packing. They even started some schools to train prospective apple pickers to replace those who one day would be too old to pick apples. Sadly, those ninety-four pickers working around the homestead began fighting among themselves. Incredible as it may sound, some began stealing apples that had already been picked. Although there were enough trees on the 10,000 acres to keep every available worker busy, those working nearest the homestead failed to move into unharvested areas. They just kept working those 800 acres nearest the house. Some on the northern edge sent their trucks to get apples on the southern side. And those on the south side sent their trucks to gather on the east side. Even with all that activity, the harvest on the remaining 9,200 acres was left to just six pickers. Those six were, of course, far too few to gather all the ripe fruit in those thousands of acres. So, by the hundreds of thousands, apples rotted on the trees and fell to the ground. One of the students at the apple-picking school showed a special talent for picking apples quickly and effectively. When he heard about the thousands of acres of untouched faraway orchards, he started talking about going there.

His friends discouraged him. They said: "Your talents and abilities make you very valuable around the homestead. You'd be wasting your talents out there. Your gifts can help us harvest apples from the trees on our central 800 acres more rapidly. That will give us more time to build bigger and better storehouses. Perhaps you could even help us devise better ways to use our big storehouses since we have wound up with more space than we need for the present crop of apples."

With so many workers and so few trees, the pickers and packers and truck drivers -- and all the rest of the Society for the Picking of Apples living around the homestead -- had time for more than just picking apples. They built nice houses and raised their standard of living. Some became very conscious of clothing styles. Thus, when the six pickers from the far-off orchards returned to the homestead for a visit, it was apparent that they were not keeping up with the styles in vogue with the other apple pickers and packers. To be sure, those on the homestead were always good to those six who worked in the far away orchards. When any of those six returned from the far away fields, they were given the red carpet treatment. Nonetheless, those six pickers were saddened that the Society of the Picking of Apples spent 96 percent of its budget for bigger and better apple-picking methods and equipment and personnel for the 800 acres around the homestead while it spent only 4 percent of its budget on all those distant orchards. To be sure, those six pickers knew that an apple is an apple wherever it may be picked. They knew that the apples around the homestead were just as important as apples far away. Still, they could not erase from their minds the sight of thousands of trees that had never been touched by a picker. They longed for more pickers to come help them. They longed for help from packers, truck drivers, supervisors, equipment-maintenance men, and ladder builders. They wondered if the professionals working back around the homestead could teach them better apple-picking methods so that, out where they worked, fewer apples would rot and fall to the ground. Those six sometimes wondered to themselves whether or not the Society for the Picking of Apples was doing what the orchard owner had asked it to do.

While one might question whether the Society was doing all that the owner wanted done, the members did keep very busy. Several members were convinced that proper apple picking requires nothing less than the very best equipment. Thus, the Society assigned several members to develop bigger and better ladders as well as nicer boxes to store apples. The Society also prided itself at having raised the qualification level for full-time apple pickers. When the owner returns, the Society members will crowd around him. They'll proudly show off the bigger and better ladders they've built and the nice apple boxes they've designed and made. One wonders how happy that owner will be, however, when he looks out and sees the acres and acres of untouched trees with their unpicked apples.[47]

Teamed Together for a Holy Purpose

Paul's effectiveness in ministry was dramatically increased because he chose not to operate alone, but within the context

213

of a team. He was with someone almost every time he set out. The New Testament mentions Barnabas, Silas, Timothy, Luke, Epaphroditus, Priscilla, Aquila and many others who personally accompanied Paul on his missionary journeys. Paul's conviction to work with others was so strong that in one of his letters, he explains:

> Now when I went to Troas to preach the gospel of Christ and found that the Lord had opened a door for me, I still had no peace of mind, because I did not find my brother Titus there. So I said goodbye to them and went on to Macedonia. (2 Corinthians 2:12-13)

Even an open door was not strong enough incentive for Paul to work alone. He did not operate alone for several reasons. One primary purpose for Paul working with others was his understanding that discipleship is better "caught" than taught. When Paul traveled, he took men along so they could learn firsthand how to operate in the Spirit of God. In addition, Paul had a clear understanding of the power of teamwork. He sought those with gifts that complemented his own, and he coordinated these people for the greater good. Even though he was an extremely gifted leader, he was not deceived into thinking that he could do everything well. He understood that he needed others and honored their God-given abilities in order to see the work of the gospel accomplished.

In the 19th century, William Carey and the "Serempore Trio" displayed Paul's style of life-giving teamwork. Although known as the Father of Modern Missions, Carey did not regard himself as particularly outstanding. He was an ordinary man, a shoemaker, who professed, "I can plod. I can persevere in any definite pursuit. To this I owe everything."[48] Another reason for Carey's success was that he labored together for many years with other persevering, albeit flawed men. This is a description of some of their achievements:

> Carey formed a team of colleagues (the Serampore Trio) whose accomplishments elevated them to first magnitude in all missions' history. Carey's team translated the Bible in 34 Asian languages, compiled dictionaries of Sanskrit, Marathi, Panjabi, and Telegu—respected even today as authoritative; started the still influential Serampore College; began churches and established 19 mission stations; formed 100 rural schools encouraging the education of girls; started the Horticultural Society of India; served as a professor at Fort William College, Calcutta; began the weekly publication "THE FRIEND OF INDIA," (continued today as "THE STATESMAN"); printed the first Indian newspaper; introduced the concept of the savings bank to assist poor farmers. His fight against the burning of widows ("SATI") helped lead to its ban in 1829. His life inspired tens of thousands to give themselves for the spread of the Gospel.[49]

Another reason that I suspect Paul valued working together with others was that it provided him much needed accountability. A modern example of holy accountability is the Modesto Manifesto, a document developed by evangelist Billy Graham:

> During his meetings in Modesto, California, in November 1948, Billy Graham met with his co-workers and friends George Beverly Shea, Grady Wilson, and Cliff Barrows (at the motel on South Ninth Street where they were staying) to determine what were the most common criticisms of evangelists and how they should organize their own meetings so

that they would be above reproach. Among the points they agreed on was that the Graham team would avoid even any appearance of financial abuse, exercise extreme care to avoid even the appearance of any sexual impropriety (from that point on, Graham made it a point not to travel, meet or eat alone with any woman other than his wife Ruth), to cooperate with any local churches that were willing to participate in united evangelism effort, and to be honest and reliable in their publicity and reporting of results.[50]

In contrast to the many public Christian figures who have struggled with integrity, Billy Graham, through the power of accountability and teamwork, was able to stay scandal-free for over fifty years. No doubt, Paul also owed much to the deep friendships he had with his less acclaimed partners in the ministry.

Accountability is not only intended to help us to stay free of sinful patterns, but to enable us to accomplish the holy mandate God has given us. The goal of the Christian life is not simply to live free of sin, but to use that freedom to advance into the darkness and deliver men from Satan's realm. One of Satan's diabolical schemes is to subtly change our goals in life. He attempts to siphon our desire to advance spiritually and leave us with a survival mentality. Persevering in life-giving accountability with godly friends helps us to consistently advance against the forces of darkness in our lives and to be a conduit of freedom for others.

Love Not our Lives Unto Death

An overarching reason that Paul had enormous impact for God's kingdom was because he did not live in fear, even fear of death itself. Paul's dear friends at the house of Phillip in

Caesarea strove to convince him not to go to Jerusalem out of fear for his life. Luke, the author of Acts and an eyewitness to the event, explains:

> *Then Paul answered, "Why are you weeping and breaking my heart? I am ready not only to be bound, but also to die in Jerusalem for the name of the Lord Jesus." When he would not be dissuaded, we gave up and said, "The Lord's will be done."* (Acts 21:13-14)

Just as Peter challenged Jesus not to go to his death, Paul underwent a similar test. Paul's reaction revealed, however, that he had already relinquished his right to life if it would bring glory to God.

For those who do not live to preserve their lives in this world, there is no limit to what God can accomplish through them. The Moravian missionaries of the eighteenth century were just such a people, an essential part of advancing the kingdom of God during that era. Beginning with a potter named Leonard Dober and a carpenter named David Nitschmann, who went to the Caribbean island of St Thomas in 1732, the Moravians reached many parts of the world, including North and South America, the Arctic, Africa, and the Far East. Sometimes they even sold themselves into slavery in order to bring the message of Christ to those they were serving. The famous cry of these missionaries became, "May the Lamb who was slain receive the reward of his suffering!"[51] In like manner, Paul's heart burned that Jesus might receive His reward in full from among the peoples of the Roman world.

Paul's wholehearted obedience to God shines as a beacon of light for us to follow. Toward the end of his life, he boldly proclaimed:

> *For I am already being poured out like a drink offering, and the time has come for my*

departure. I have fought the good fight, I have finished the race, I have kept the faith. Now there is in store for me the crown of righteousness, which the Lord, the righteous Judge, will award to me on that day - and not only to me, but also to all who have longed for his appearing. (2 Timothy 4:6-8)

In our day, the apostolic zeal that characterized Paul's life is being restored not merely to individuals, but to the church as a whole. God's express intent is that all nations may hear the testimony of the risen Christ. Only then will the end of this age come. Paul finished his race of hastening the Lord's return. The question each of us must face is, "What can we do to bring this apostolic task to completion in our generation?"

SECTION 15

JESUS – THE GREAT GOD OF MEN

Learn to know Christ and him crucified. Learn to sing to him, and say, "Lord Jesus, you are my righteousness, I am your sin. You have taken upon yourself what is mine and given me what is yours. You have become what you were not so that I might become what I was not.
- Martin Luther

To comment fully upon the Lord Jesus in a few pages is a futile effort. John the Beloved, speaking about the limitations of his own account about Christ, commented, "*Jesus did many other things as well. If every one of them were written down, I suppose that even the whole world would not have room for the books that would be written*" (John 21:25). Jesus is both the great God of men and the great Man of God. He is the ultimate fulfillment of what we glimpse in those who we have studied in this book. Looking at the Lord Jesus, we must stand back and worship Him who came to die for rebellious ones and rose again to reign forever with them. As the word of God expresses so clearly, Jesus appeared to destroy the devil's work (1 John 3:8), and through the cross He surely did! As we look at some of the attributes of the Lord Jesus, may we see Him more clearly than ever before, and may we be fully obedient to His holy will for the rest of our lives.

CHAPTER 30

SERVANT OF ALL, SAVIOR OF THE WORLD

Servant of All

Humility is beautiful in God's sight. Those who are humble are the truly great ones in God's kingdom, and those who are arrogant cannot have a place before God. Jesus, through whom all things were made (John 1:2), exhibited humility in His every word and deed. He came to earth and lived His life with simplicity. Paul, writing to the Philippians about what true humility is, elaborates on the choice the Son of God made to humble himself:

> *Each of you should look not only to your own interests, but also to the interests of others. Your attitude should be the same as that of Christ Jesus: Who, being in very nature God, did not consider equality with God something to be grasped, but made himself nothing, taking the very nature of a servant, being made in human likeness. And being found in appearance as a man, he humbled himself and became obedient to death - even death on a cross!* (Philippians 2:4-8)

Jesus has never committed a selfish act; He embodies the true nature of humility. He is not tainted with a propensity toward false motives like the rest of us. Jesus knows who He is, and out of that knowledge He serves. God leads sincere believers to increasingly exhibit that same kind of profound security in their own motives and actions. John's gospel reads:

> *It was just before the Passover Feast. Jesus knew that the time had come for him to leave this world and go to the Father. Having loved*

his own who were in the world, he now show-
ed them the full extent of his love. The evening
meal was being served, and the devil had
already prompted Judas Iscariot, son of
Simon, to betray Jesus. Jesus knew that the
Father had put all things under his power, and
that he had come from God and was returning
to God; so he got up from the meal, took off
his outer clothing, and wrapped a towel
around his waist. After that, he poured water
into a basin and began to wash his disciples'
feet, drying them with the towel that was
wrapped around him. (John 13:1-5)

Jesus, the greatest man who ever lived, served His disciples by washing their feet. We must seriously contemplate
this radical, unexpected, and symbolic act. We will not be able
to serve God adequately unless we see that He has served us
first. It is his nature to serve; He has set the example, and we
will never be able to outdo Him. John Dawson contrasted
Christ's way of leading with the world's way when he said,
"God does not primarily relate to us through his authority."[52]
Although people enjoy throwing their weight around to prove
their position and power, Jesus is completely different from
any leader we have ever known. He is able to serve because
He is secure in His position with the Father. He is unmatched
in strength and power, yet He wins our love through humility.

A marvelous man of God, Travis Gibson, demonstrated to
me the "downward mobility" of Christ's servant leadership
style. He was the pastor of visitation at Highland Baptist
Church in Waco, Texas, which I attended in the 1990s. He was
an elderly man when I first met him, and he went to be with
the Lord several years ago. A distinguishing mark of Gibson
was the Christ-like humility he expressed in all that he did.
What a lovely man he was, so full of God's kindness and energy! His life was given to loving God and serving the broken

and hurting. Church membership did not matter to him; he loved all who crossed his path. He sat with people in their most disheartening and difficult times, many times in hospitals and funeral homes, comforting them and carrying their burdens before God. Day after day, year after year, he and his wife Juanita cared for people with God's unending love. This man was an example of humility to all who knew him and was recognized to be a man of unyielding obedience.

When people would ask him about his motivation for ministry, Gibson would share about a time the Lord showed him a vision. Young and fresh out of seminary, he was pastoring a small Baptist church in Texas. An opportunity arose for him to pastor a larger Baptist church and he applied for the position, but to his disappointment he did not get it. Gibson told the Lord how discouraged he was, saying, "Here I am serving you, climbing the ladder." At that moment, he saw before him a hole in the ground and the top of a ladder sticking out. He was pondering what this could mean when the Lord spoke to him about this picture, "Travis, the ladder in My kingdom goes down." As a result of this dream, Gibson spent the remainder of his life seeking to walk in humility before God and man. He was not concerned about titles or positions, but about the people whom God had created and loved. Imitating his beloved Redeemer, Gibson cared for others with the hope of Christ's promise, *"Whoever wants to be great among you must be your servant, and whoever wants to be first must be the slave of all"* (Mark 10:43-44).

Savior

Unless we know the bad news regarding our sinfulness, we will not appreciate the good news of salvation through Jesus Christ. One of the key hindrances to people accepting the forgiveness of Jesus is that they do not appreciate the severity of their situation before God. When people say, "I am basically a good person" or "There are many ways to God," it reveals a lack of understanding about their true heart condition. From the moment Adam and Eve sinned in the Garden of Eden, humans have been separated from God and twisted by sin. Although for many it takes time to realize their desperate condition, we all, as inheritors of Adam and Eve's nature, are in danger of the most severe eternal torment through our separation from God. Some know they deserve punishment for things they have done, and yet, nothing could make up for our transgressions against God. We all are without excuse. With this backdrop of our sinfulness, the gospel ("good news") is seen for what it is.

God has made a way for us to be free from the eternal punishment our sin merits. The Old Testament reveals clues about the new way that was to supersede the old one of law and judgment. Here is one such prophetic hint: a woman once spoke to King David regarding his son Absalom, who had been banished after he rebelled against David and attempted to take over the kingdom. In her words, we see a beautiful picture of the heart of God that was fully expressed in the coming of Jesus to earth. She says:

> *Like water spilled on the ground, which cannot be recovered, so we must die. But God does not take away life; instead, he devises ways so that a banished person may not remain estranged from him.* (2 Samuel 14:14)

What a high view of God we see in this passage, a view ultimately manifested in the Christ. God devised a way to be reconciled to man. In the wisdom of God, He found a way to do away with our sin and to bring our banished souls back to Him. We should pause to worship our loving God because of His mercy.

Once, while returning from a trip to Asia, my wife and I spoke to a fellow passenger on the plane about Jesus. He began with a familiar argument by asking me why God could allow such suffering and evil on earth. I explained to him that it is not God who is on trial; man is on trial for his rebellion and disobedience. From the very beginning of the human race, God has made clear to man the consequences of sin, and He has every right to banish us forever from His holy presence. But God, in His justice and infinite wisdom, sent Jesus to pay the penalty for our sin. If this fact has lost its luster in our hearts, we should ask God to forgive us and reveal the beauty of our salvation once again. Isaiah prophesies of Jesus:

> *Surely he took up our infirmities and carried our sorrows, yet we considered him stricken by God, smitten by him, and afflicted. But he was pierced for our transgressions, he was crushed for our iniquities; the punishment that brought us peace was upon him, and by his wounds we are healed. We all, like sheep, have gone astray, each of us has turned to his own way; and the LORD has laid on him the iniquity of us all.* (Isaiah 53:4-6)

Man opened the door to Satan's kingdom through disobedience to God's holy command. As a result, suffering and pain have come. Human wisdom prefers denying culpability for our sin. However, our King paid the ultimate price so that suffering and sin would be destroyed forever. Jesus did not die simply to make our lives better, He died to purchase men for God and rescue us from the flames of hell. He did not die out of duty, but for the joy set before Him; He died to give us a place with Him in His kingdom. Jesus is not a "happy pill" designed to make our lives better; He is a holy Savior who demands our complete allegiance. There is coming a day when all that is wrong will be made right and Jesus will stand victorious on the earth. Sin and death will be thrown into the lake of fire forever, and the Father, Son and Holy Spirit will rule in righteousness and justice forevermore.

CHAPTER 31

OUR JOYOUS KING

King of Kings

Jeremiah exclaimed, *"Who should not revere you, O King of the nations? This is your due. Among all the wise men of the nations and in all their kingdoms, there is no one like you"* (Jeremiah 10:7). He was prophesying of our Lord Jesus, who is far above all in power, wisdom and majesty. Echoing Jeremiah's praise, the late preacher Dr. S.M. Lockridge gave one of the best descriptions of Jesus that I have ever heard. An excerpt of his sermon entitled "My King" expresses well the completeness of Jesus' kingship. Dr. Lockridge speaks with his beautiful, gravelly voice and exclaims:

> My King was born King. The
> Bible says He's a Seven Way
> King. He's the King of the
> Jews – that's a racial King.
> He's the King of Israel –
> that's a National King. He's
> the King of righteousness.
> He's the King of the ages.
> He's the King of Heaven.
> He's the King of glory. He's
> the King of kings and He is
> the Lord of lords. Now that's
> my King. Well I wonder
> if you know him. Do you
> know him?[53]

Dr. Lockridge caught a glimpse of the King in all His glory. When the clouds part on the day Jesus returns with His angels, every one who sees Him will be overwhelmingly surprised. No one will be exempt from awe in His presence.

Those who have performed evil will shrink away in everlasting fear and dread. Those who have promoted righteousness will marvel with joy that the Lord Jesus is greater than they could have ever imagined. An Old Testament clue about this kind of awe is described when the Queen of Sheba visited Israel's King Solomon. The biblical account states:

> When the queen of Sheba saw all the wisdom of Solomon and the palace he had built, the food on his table, the seating of his officials, the attending servants in their robes, his cupbearers, and the burnt offerings he made at the temple of the LORD, she was overwhelmed. She said to the king, "The report I heard in my own country about your achievements and your wisdom is true. But I did not believe these things until I came and saw with my own eyes. Indeed, not even half was told me; in wisdom and wealth you have far exceeded the report I heard." (1 Kings 10:4-9)

Her breath was taken away when she saw him, and he far exceeded her expectations. This foreshadows the day when we see Jesus and breathlessly fall at his feet in worship.

The Oil of Joy Above His Brothers

Those who view Jesus as surly and sour are not in touch with the Lord and Savior we see in scripture. One of the greatest misconceptions regarding Jesus in all of Christendom is His joyful heart. I continually remind our congregation in Boston that God is not a killjoy; He is a "givejoy." The writer to the Hebrews, quoting Psalm 45:7, states: *"You have loved righteousness and hated lawlessness; Therefore God, Your God, has anointed You with the oil of gladness more than Your companions"* (Hebrews 1:9-NKJV). Jesus had greater joy than anyone on the face of the earth. No one wants to be around a stoic, who does not know how to enjoy life. We can be sure that the disciples were astounded at the joy that emanated from their friend and leader.

The people at Bethel Church in Redding, California, describe it this way, "God is in a good mood." Although Jesus' heart was broken over sin, and He was grieved at people's hardness of heart, He was a man who experienced life to the full. When Jesus said, *"The thief comes only to steal and kill and destroy; I have come that they may have life, and have life to the full"* (John 10:10), He was contrasting the effect of following Him with the consequence of following the evil one. In order to follow Jesus, we must take the narrow road, but as we obey Him we find that we are not restricted in our hearts. We are increasingly free from the control of sin and the bondage to destructive attitudes and desires. We are truly able to enjoy the life God has given us. In contrast, when people follow the path on which Satan is travelling, the road is wide. However, after they continue on this path for a time, they become restricted in heart; vice, fear, shame, bitterness, jealousy and a host of other complexities impede their ability to experience love, peace and joy. They are unable to enjoy the abundant life that God generously gives to those whose hope is in Him.

A misconception exists in the Western world because we refuse to see suffering and joy going together hand in hand. In the minds of many believers, these two concepts are diametrically opposed. We have a hard time believing it is possible to walk in joy if we are going through trial and suffering. Often, our idea of being "blessed" expects a lack of problems and an abundance of tangible benefits, such as money and possessions. But, this is not a biblical idea. Jesus suffered loss more than anyone in history, and yet, in contrast to this reality, the scripture clearly explains that He was more blessed with joy than anyone who has ever lived.

Joy and pain were companions in the life of Samuel Zwemer, known to many as the "Apostle to Islam." He was a living example of the joy of God through intense suffering. Zwemer left America as a missionary for Arabia in June 1890. In July 1904, two daughters of Samuel and his wife Amy succumbed to dysentery on the island of Bahrain, dying within eight days of each other. In an article in the *International Journal of Frontier Missions*, Dr. J Christy Wilson recounts how the sorrowing parents inscribed on their daughter's gravestones, "WORTHY IS THE LAMB WHO WAS SLAIN TO RECEIVE RICHES." Then, in 1937, Zwemer lost his beloved wife. In 1950, he lost his second wife, Margaret. Zwemer's converts in the Muslim world were less than a dozen in over forty years of ministry in that region. Yet through all of this intense suffering, he was known to have a joyous spirit. After fifty years of labor, he said, "The sheer joy of it all comes back. Gladly I would do it all over again."[54] For the passionate follower of Jesus, the greatest joy is always ahead. At his advanced age, Zwemer looked forward with anticipation to heaven, where he had stored his reward. This is an important life lesson for us: In order to walk in consistent joy, we must live with the hope of our reward in eternity. As we walk with Jesus, the joyous one, even in the midst of great trials, He will make our joy complete (John 15:11, 16:14).

God with Us

The overarching theme of the biblical message is God redeeming mankind so that He may be with us again. In Isaiah 7:14, the prophet writes that the name of the Messiah will be "Immanuel," which means "God with us." This is a crucial distinction in our faith in Christ, our Messiah, when compared to mere religious ritual. The difference between religion and relationship with God is that in religion, God is distant and His presence is delayed and distant. But in relationship, God is right here, right now. Jesus died to purchase us so that we may live our lives with the holy expectation that God is here now. At present, God meets with us through the veil of the flesh. When the clouds part, however, and Jesus returns, we will meet Him face-to-face, marveling at His greatness (2 Thessalonians 1:7-10) and reveling in His goodness.

There are many competing affections in this world that are poor substitutes for the real and living God. We are not great in ourselves, but we are greatly loved, and as a result, we are great in Him. He is mighty and He is full of mercy. Let us give the rest of our lives to know and be known by the Great God of Men.

EPILOGUE

The only hope of a decreasing self is an increasing Christ.
- F.B. Meyer, English author and Baptist pastor

In 1985, the leadership of Highland Baptist Church in Waco, Texas, fragmented and scattered. But some, like Associate Pastor Mark Wible, remained at Highland to help guide the church through the painful transition. Wible had a dream one night. He saw a huge piece of machinery with a wrecking ball on it next to the original sanctuary. The building had already gone through multiple renovations and additions, and the sanctuary was converted into an education building. In Wible's dream, the wrecking ball hit the building and it fell to the ground. A wind then swept away the rubble and dust, and Mark saw the letters J-E-S-U-S chiseled into the foundation. Then he heard a voice, "Now, build on this foundation." A couple of days later, a storm came through Waco at night, lightning struck this same building and a fire swept through it. In the aftermath, a professional demolition crew used a wrecking ball to tear the remainder of the building down. What a profound message God was sending. In the years leading up to the fall of the key leader, high-profile personalities and ambitious plans were laid, with many of man's additions to the gospel, but the foundation was not laid solely on Jesus. When the leadership fell apart, numerous people's hopes were dashed and many people were hurt. The time had come for this church to build on Jesus alone.

I am reminded of a life built upon the foundation of Jesus that stood firm through the storms of life. Anne O'leary's love for her Savior was a testimony to all. I met Anne and her husband Tom in the spring of 1990, and we eventually developed a deep friendship. Anne had been diagnosed with multiple sclerosis several years before we met, and by that time she used a scooter to move around in her home. Tom was one of the most selfless examples I have seen of a faithful and loving husband, and Anne was one of the most Christ-like people that

I have ever encountered. One of the things that first struck me about Anne was her deep reservoir of love. She enjoyed praying for those who were pregnant and fervently sought God for those who went to preach the gospel on the mission field.

In the summer of 1990, while I was in Thailand preaching the gospel, I received a letter from Anne. As I read the letter that she had written with her own hand, I was dumbstruck. Due to Anne's feeble physical condition, the writing was large and crooked. It was evident that she had labored over the letter for quite some time. God's goodness shone through as I read her words encouraging me to serve God with all of my heart, and explaining that she was praying for me. Anne did not meditate on what she could not do, but on the One who could do all things through her (Philippians 4:13). Soon after that summer, Anne grew worse and became confined to a wheelchair. One day, as she was at church, we began to sing a Dennis Jernigan song entitled, *I Stand Amazed*. She motioned to her husband that she wanted to stand in the presence of the Lord and a friend, Tim Flanagan, and I had the honor of helping her stand as she offered this sacrifice of praise to God.

Not long after that experience, she was bedridden and was unable to do anything for herself. Tom told me a story during this time that exemplifies a life given to the Savior. One evening, Tom had washed Anne, put her to bed, and was out in the living room spending time with Jesus. As he was seeking the Lord, he heard Anne violently coughing and having uncontrollable spasms. His heart broke and he went straightaway to tend to her. He approached the door of the room and heard her praying, *for him*. She was concerned not for herself, but she was concerned that her husband Tom would be okay in the midst of this trial. Anne was a living picture of our Lord and Savior Jesus Christ when He suffered on the cross for our sins. Because Anne was captivated with her Savior, she was overflowing with His love. Anne is presently jumping and dancing in the presence of the Lord. When I pass through the doors to everlasting life, I will gladly join her in celebrating Him who bore our sin.

These stories illustrate the heart of this book. We must remain focused on the One who enables God's greatness to live in us. As life progresses, things seem to become more complicated, but it is paramount that we return to the simplicity of our relationship with Jesus. With ever-increasing responsibilities at home, at work, and in the church, we must learn to practice God's presence in the midst of them, lest we succumb to discouragement or drift into worldly thinking and living. If we rely on Jesus, we will be empowered by His everlasting commitment to us. Then, when all is said and done, we will hear the voice of the great God of men saying, *"Well done, good and faithful servant! You have been faithful with a few things; I will put you in charge of many things. Come and share your master's happiness!"* (Matthew 25:23).

NOTES

1. Tucker, Ruth A. *From Jerusalem to Irian Jaya.* Grand Rapids, MI: Zondervan, 2004. (pg. 311)

2. Pullinger, Jackie with Quicke,Andrew, *Chasing the Dragon.* Ventura, CA: Regal, 2001.

3. Vanauken, Sheldon *A Severe Mercy,* San Francisco, CA: Harper, San Francisco, 1980.

4. Nee, Watchman *Spiritual Authority* New York, NY: Christian Fellwship, 1972. (pg. 94)

5. Taylor, Dr. & Mrs. *Hudson Taylor's Spiritual Secret* , Chicago, IL: Moody Bible Institute, 1989. (pg. 202)

6. Sherman, Dean, perf. *Spiritual Warfare for Every Christian.* Crown Ministries International, 1996. DVD.

7. Rose, Darlene *I Will Never Leave Thee I-III.* Focus On The Family Radio Broadcast, Compact Disc. CBD Stock No: WW5008888

8. Wimber, John *Signs, Wonders and Church Growth Video Series* Anaheim, CA: Vineyard, 1984. Video Cassette.

9. Curry, Dayna & Mercer, Heather with Mattingly, Stacy *Prisoners of Hope,* New York, NY: Doubleday, 2002.

10. Johnson, Bill. "How do I increase in a lifestyle of miracles?." Bill Johnson Ministries. N.p., n.d. Web. June 28, 2012. <http://www.bjm.org/questions/3/how-do-i-increase-in-a-lifestyle-of-miracles.html>.

11. Hattingh, Suzette, perf. Intercession as a Lifestyle. Voice in the City, 1997. Film.

12. Specter, Michael. "The Long Ride: How Did Lance Armstrong Manage the Greatest Comeback in Sports History?." New Yorker. July 15, 2002: 48-58. Print.

13. C.T., Studd. "Rescue Station at the Gates of Hell." Sermon. Available at http://www.theoldtimegospel.org

14. Frangipane, Francis. *The Three Battlegrounds*. Grand Rapids: Arrow Publications, 1977. (pg. 16)

15. Niebuhr, Gustav. Washington Post 4 February 1994, n. pag. Print.

16. Kierkegaard, Soren. *Purity of Heart is to Will One Thing*. Radford: A&D Publishing, 2008. Print.

17. Green, Keith, perf. To Obey is Better Than Sacrifice. Universal Music, MGB Songs International, 1978. Song.

18. Scriven, Joseph, perf. What a Friend We Have in Jesus, 1855. Song.

19. Popenoe, Paul & Johnson, Roswell. *Applied Eugenics*. New York: The Macmillan Company, 1918 (pg 162).

20. Manser, Martin H., *The Westminster Collection of Christian Quotations*. Louisville, Westminster John Knox Press, 2001. (pg 8).

21. The Free Online Dictionary, http://www.thefreedictionary.com

22. Muller, George. *The Autobiography of George Muller*. Pittsburgh: Whitaker House, 1984.

23. Piper, John. *Let The Nations Be Glad.* Grand Rapids: Baker Academic, 2003. (pg 45)

24. Sherman, Dean, perf. Spiritual Warfare for Every Christian. Crown Ministries International, 1996. DVD.

25. Wimber, John Signs, Wonders and Church Growth Video Series. Anaheim, CA: Vineyard, 1984. Video Cassette

26. Dawson, John, perf. Father Heart of God. Last Days Ministries, Unsure of Date. Video Cassette.

27. Caedmon's Call, perf. This World. Brentwood, 2004. Song.

28. Quotations from Borden of Yale '09: "The Life that Counts", Mrs. Howard Taylor; China Inland Mission, 1913. Moody Press, Chicago - Portions based on material in *Daily Bread,* December 31, 1988, and *The Yale Standard*, Fall 1970 edition.

29. Hill, E.V. "Sunday's Coming." Mt. Zion Missionary Baptist Church. Los Angeles. Sermon.

30. Ellis, William Thomas. *Billy Sunday, The Man and His Message.* Philadelphia: John C. Winston Company Publishers, 1927. (pg 277)

31. Day, Doris, perf. Que Sera, Sera (Whatever Will Be, Will Be). Columbia Records, 1956. Song.

32. Hattingh, Suzette, perf. Intercession as a Lifestyle. Voice in the City, 1997. Film.

33. Miller, Basil. *John Wesley.* Minneapolis: Bethany House Publishers, 1973. (pg 53)

34. Billheimer, Paul. *Love Covers*. Fort Washington: Christian Literature Crusade, 1981. (pg 106,107)

35. Collins, Glenn. "A Family, a Feud and a Six-Foot Sandwich." New York Times [New York] 8 December 2001, n. pag. Web. 28 Jun. 2012. <http://www.nytimes.com/2001/12/08/nyregion/a-family-a-feud-and-a-six-foot-sandwich.html?pagewanted=all>.

36. Bonnke, Reinhardt. *Evangelism by Fire: Keys for effectively reaching others with the gospel*. Lake Mary: Charisma House, 2011.

37. Stedman, Ray. *Talking with My Father: Jesus Teaches on Prayer*. Grand Rapids: Discovery House Publishers, 1997. (pg 27,28)

38. Green, Keith, perf. There is a Redeemer, Birdwing Music, BMG Songs, Ears To Hear Music. 1982.

39. Bickle, Mike & Hiebert, Deborah. *The 7 Longings of the Human Heart*. Kansas City: Forerunner Books, 2006. (pg 8)

40. "Quotes of Leonard Ravenhill" Web. June 28, 2012. http://www.gospeltruth.net/ravenhill.htm

41. Bevere, John. *Driven By Eternity: Making Your Life Count Today & Forever*. New York: Time Warner Book Group, 2006. (pgs ix and x)

42. Powers, Barbara Hudson. *The Henrietta Mears Story*. Old Tapan: Fleming H. Revell Company, 1957.

43. Elliot, Elizabeth. *Shadow of the Almighty: The Life and*

Testament of Jim Elliot (Lives of Faith). New York: Harper Collins, 1958. (pg 59)

44. Cymbala, Jim. *Fresh Wind, Fresh Fire*. Grand Rapids: Zondervan Publishing House, 1997. (pg 125,126)

45. Allen, Roland. *Missionary Methods: St. Paul's or Ours?*. Grand Rapids: World Dominion Press, 1962. (pg 74)

46. . "Lewis and Clark: American Explorers." Enchanted Learning. N.p., n.d. Web. June 28, 2012. <http://www.enchantedlearning.com/explorers/page/l/lewi sandclark.shtml>.

47. Original version appeared in *Let's Quit Kidding Ourselves About Missions*, Moody Press. © 1979 by The Moody Bible Institute. Edited and revised by Howard Culbertson.

48. Tucker, Ruth A. *From Jerusalem to Irian Jaya*. Grand Rapids, MI: Zondervan, 2004. (pg. 122)

49. Severance, Dr. Diane. "William Carey's Amazing Mission." Christianity.com. N.p., n.d. Web. June 28, 2012. <http://www.enchantedlearning.com/explorers/page/l/lewi sandclark.shtml>.

50. . "What part did the Modesto Manifesto play in the ministry of Billy Graham?." Billy Graham Center. BGC Archives, January 31, 2007. Web. June 28, 2012. <www.wheaton.edu/bgc/archives/faq/4.htm>.

51. Reidhead, Paris. "Ten Shekels and a Shirt." Paris Reidhead Bible Teaching Ministries. N.p., n.d. Web. June 28, 2012.

<http://www.parisreidheadbibleteachingministries.org/ten shekels.shtml>.

52. Dawson, John, perf. Father Heart of God. Last Days Ministries. Video Cassette.

53. Shadrach Meshach Lockridge (March 7, 1913 – April 4, 2000) was the Pastor of Calvary Baptist Church, a prominent African-American congregation located in San Diego, California, from 1953 to 1993. Dibble, Sandra (April 8, 2000), San Diego Union-Tribune.

54. Wilson, J. Christy, International Journal of Christian Missions, October - December 1996, Vol. 13, No. 4

55. Tucker, Ruth A. *From Jerusalem to Irian Jaya*. Grand Rapids, MI: Zondervan, 2004. (pg 240)

Made in the USA
Charleston, SC
23 August 2012